Praise

'I love the introspection throughout this book; it's one part therapy, one part leadership. So many books try to do the second without addressing the first.'
— **Joan Colletta**, Senior Director Global Brand Marketing, McDonald's Corp

'An invigorating read that draws parallels between the fundamentals of leadership with elements of nature. Fire symbolises purpose-driven leadership, fuel denotes talent and cash, and oxygen epitomises market dynamics. This book will guide you through a systemic and emphatic approach to make your leadership a transformative force.'
— **Umang Vohra**, Managing Director and Global CEO, Cipla Ltd

'Transformative, thought-provoking and packed with real-world insights and interviews.'
— **Sarala Menon**, EVP, E2E Supply Chain, Colgate Palmolive India and South Asia

'Packed with real-world insights, *Disruptive Leadership* provides the blueprint for transformative and sustainable leadership. A masterclass in driving change with purpose.'
— **Dame Inga Beale**, Portfolio Director and former CEO of Lloyd's of London

'Filled with true business examples, creative analogies and managerial insights rarely mentioned in leadership literature. Thought provoking and offers clear-headed guidance for any type of leader facing disruptive leadership challenges.

— **Zoran Bogdanovic**, CEO, Coca-Cola Hellenic

'In this book, riveting narratives inspiring stories of pioneering leaders come alive, paired with transformative insight and exercises. It's not just about challenging the norm; it's about reimagining 'success' personally and profoundly. Essential reading for todays' changemakers.'

— **Audrey Clegg**, Chief Talent Officer, Sanofi S.A.

'This book is a game-changer. Drawing parallels with fire is not only innovative but brilliantly insightful.'

— **Mehrnavaz Avari**, Area Director UK and GM, Taj 51 Buckingham Gate Suites and Residences (part of The Indian Hotels Company)

'From the first page, *Disruptive Leadership* sparks a transformative journey. It's not just a book; it's a leadership manifesto for our times. Every leader should delve into its wisdom.'

— **Segun Ogunsanya**, Group CEO/Managing Director, Airtel Africa plc

DISRUPTIVE LEADERSHIP

USING FIRE TO DRIVE PURPOSEFUL CHANGE

MARK BATEMAN

R^ethink

First published in Great Britain in 2024
by Rethink Press (www.rethinkpress.com)

© Copyright Mark Bateman

Contents

Foreword

Disruptors are a breed apart. From the prehistoric inventor who sculpted the first wheel, to Marie Curie who pioneered our understanding of radioactivity, or Michelangelo planning his first brushstrokes in the Sistine Chapel – we owe a great part of our progress as a civilisation to disruptors who were simply not satisfied with the status quo.

Are disruptors born, or are they made?

It is a bit of both.

Having worked with CEOs around the world, Mark has had the uncommon opportunity to watch the methods of many iconic leaders closely. He has spent hundreds of hours working with, coaching and interviewing leaders, and distilling their stories into clear, tangible, practical insights.

I have the joy of being one of the Executive Interviewers for the WeQual Awards – that's how I first met Mark. We discovered a shared passion for empowering others in order to drive lasting, purposeful change. We share a mutual respect for driving equality and a level playing field, especially for those traditionally underrepresented in leadership cadres. So, when he told me about this book on disruptive leadership, I gladly agreed to write its foreword. Many business lessons are learned in the 'fog of war', but Mark's book is both a guide and a tool to help navigate the ups and downs that every leader, including myself, has had to face.

The world expects more from businesses today. Your employees, stakeholders, investors and customers expect more from you. And every morning, you wake up with a long list of tasks to complete or goals to accomplish. Every leader must have a certain *fire* in their belly, that drives them to do more. But, when that heat cools, what can we do to stoke it into flames again? Or what if the fire burns so strong that it burns you out, and everything around you?

While every lesson in this book is important, Chapter 6 on continued learning resonated most deeply with me. The ability to stay humble yet curious, this quality of lifelong learning is the only way to remain relevant and effective as a leader. Because a leadership role is not an end in itself. If we're not *listening* and learning every day, we're doing a grave injustice to the position we occupy.

Just like every leader I know, I spend the majority of my waking hours at work or thinking about work. There are days when I love it and days when I am challenged and exhausted by it. But at the end of the day, I want to know that all that time, effort and commitment has made a difference. That's what *Disruptive Leadership* does. Whether you're the founder of a bootstrapped start-up or the leader of a multi-billion-dollar enterprise, this is a handbook to teach you how to nourish the disruptor in you. You'll learn how to tap into your motivation again and direct the energy towards productivity. But most importantly, this book will show you how to disrupt with purpose and impact.

Thierry Delaporte, CEO and Managing Director, Wipro

Preface

I was starving as the mercury hit 28 degrees in the muggy central London garden. We'd been at our friend's house for what felt like hours, but there was still no sign of the main event. I'd glimpsed a mountain of meat in the kitchen as we'd walked through on our way outside but, concerningly, the barbeque had yet to be lit. Our host had spent a large amount of time constructing his barbecue and was clearly proud of his efforts. The full width of the base had been covered with briquettes, above which had been placed two parallel strips of 1cm wide lighter blocks that were emitting a faint whiff of kerosene. Above these he had placed more briquettes, all at a perfect parallel. It was a highly engineered work of art. All that was required was the ceremonial lighting.

The small group of assembled guests were unashamedly excited as the host struck one of his extra-long matches and easily set light to the white kerosene strips. Before long, flames rose, licking between the edges of the briquettes, and guests (me especially) watched with childlike interest. Some minutes later, it was clear that all was not well. The lighter material had burned too quickly, and the briquettes sat cold. Disaster hung in the air. One look at our host confirmed that he was panicking.

Recovering himself, he reached for reinforcements, which came in the shape of a nearby box of extra-large lighting blocks. He was clearly aware that all eyes were on him as he carefully placed them down and lit them, before piling briquettes above them. The new design for the reconstructed fire was less precise than before and much more condensed. This meant the lighter blocks lasted for longer and generated more heat. It still wasn't enough, though.

At this point, the group began to make some rather unkind remarks as to our host's skillset and experience. The would-be chef would not be beaten, though. Defiantly, and with a theatrical flourish for the starved and increasingly baying crowd, he dumped an entire bag of briquettes on top of what was already there. These briquettes came with inbuilt lighting cubes and, as the outside wrapping quickly caught fire, large flames rose. There were a few murmurs of approval, but the reaction was muted. The fire was clearly not doing what it was supposed to, but it was hard to tell because the barbeque was now encased with thick smoke. This was taking too long.

By now, the host had a look of grim determination. He was not even bothering to respond to the banter that went to and fro among the guests. He walked into the house and returned seconds later with a vacuum cleaner. The faint flicker of a smile showed that he believed he had the solution. The *pièce de résistance*. He set the vacuum cleaner motor in reverse, so it blew instead of sucked, and aimed it at the base of flames. What was a slowly burning mass of smoking briquettes became a living, raging (and contained, fortunately) inferno. A cheer rose up among the crowd as the host snapped off the vacuum with a big grin of self-satisfaction. *I make fire!* A few minutes later and the whole barbeque was a beautiful glowing red.

The event became a great success. Much meat was cooked, wine consumed and laughter shared. Each guest left full and happy after an enjoyable and memorable evening. But it was the fire that made it into this book. Why?

Watching my host struggle with his barbeque, I got to thinking about fire, and my search for a quick but powerful analogy to help leaders think differently and achieve truly disruptive change was over. When coaching leaders on a one-to-one basis, one of my central messages had always been about helping them find their purpose. It was, and still is, my firm belief that finding our true purpose can help us realise our full potential, something that is particularly important for any leader who is looking to make real change. At this barbeque, I saw that message wrapped up in a simple but powerful analogy.

Achieving your purpose is much like starting a fire.

7

Introduction

F ires can be positive or negative, constructive or destructive. In all cases, though, fire is uncompromising. It's a real force and if you are not careful, you will, of course, get badly burned.

All leaders want to ignite their chosen market, but many find themselves with a fire that splutters, spits and smokes a lot but leaves their team cold and unfulfilled. At the other end of the scale, what team wants to be led by an out-of-control wildfire that is simply too hot to manage? The best-case scenario is for a leader to have fire in their belly, igniting others with their vision for the future, and for the resulting fire to be contained by a clear set of values and intended to achieve a desired purpose.

The barbeque I mentioned in the preface and the thought process it inspired, came at a particularly interesting point in my life. I had been a leadership coach for more than a decade, working with hundreds of leaders from organisations of all sizes and stages. I'd worked with everyone from individual senior leaders of small startups to global CEOs, as well as hundreds of leadership teams. The leaders I coached hailed from marketing agencies to pharma companies, from the financial sector to manufacturing giants. My coaching career sounded impressive and my friends would regularly commend me on my apparent success. But I was frustrated. I didn't feel I was having the success, nor the impact, that I desired. What's more, I seemed to lurch between periods of feast and famine frequently.

Most recently, I had been running a successful startup called Engage Coach International, which pioneered an innovative mindset diagnostic tool that analysed how thoughts, beliefs and attitudes drive performance. I say it was successful, but despite being a good, solid, well-received business, it was not achieving anything like the turnover one would expect, and I felt I had lost my way. To cap it all, I had been working stupidly long hours for as long as I could remember and was utterly exhausted (a case of it being easier to coach a CEO than be a CEO). Something had to give. I had decided to take a sabbatical to re-assess. After more than a decade of warning other executives about the danger of burnout, I was duty-bound to listen to my own advice.

For the first few days of my sabbatical, I was a wreck. I had to practically force myself out of the house each morning. Once I did, I would walk around London with no particular destination in mind and no agenda. Most days I would end up in one of the Royal Parks, or on a bench on the Regent's Canal towpath. I would sit down, soaking up the sunshine. As the days became weeks and I walked, ran, read and meditated, I began to feel better. Even looking at a tree was a magical experience: within its branches and leaves was an entire thriving ecosystem of insects and birds, all connected to a wider universe. I spent more and more time each day reflecting (some would call it meditation).

Within a month, I felt like I had been hitched up to a nuclear power station. My energy levels were off the scale. It was not the sort of energy you get after an invigorating session at the gym. It was a more vibrant energy that comes with being truly alive. I felt more connected to myself than ever before. To many people this may sound a little alternative, but it's hard to explain how invigorating it was to actually *see* energy and its flows. By taking time out, I was soaking up all this energy. What's more, by gaining energy, I was also gaining time. I was re-energised and in love with life again.

My newfound energy allowed me to see things in a completely different way – hence the revelation at my friend's barbeque. Excited by the idea, I began to develop the idea of fire and leadership. How could I use this analogy to help more leaders? What were the elements required to make this work?

My thoughts turned to leaders I admired. Those who had clearly already found their purpose and were making their mark. What did they have that others didn't? What was it that made them stand out from the crowd and succeed? It was then that I recognised the missing ingredient. It was the thing I'd had to step out of my comfort zone to find: energy. Disruptors are often unpredictable and act way outside of the norms, but that's what gets things done. They do this because they long for, and see, a different future (their purpose), decide that they are the person to make it happen (make a difference) and expend their *energy* to bring it about.

In short, when we become consumed with purpose (the difference you want to see), it releases energy that brings that purpose to fruition. The greater the sense of purpose, the more energy is released.

Energy is infectious. To change the world, seemingly boundless supplies of energy are required. A good supply of energy can achieve unrivalled disruption. Attend any disruptive conference and feel the energy in the room. Pick any of the latest hot topics – cryptocurrencies, smart contracts, artificial intelligence, gene manipulation, medtech – the energy around them drives a desire to solve real problems, to be the first and the best, to make money or simply experience the pure joy of innovation. The energy generated by and in these spaces could run a country. It's hard not to be inspired when you're around people burning with purpose and excitement, whether they are young or old, formally educated or not.

Energy makes change happen. Across the world you'll find people under pressure. Marginalised. Angry.

Heated. Black Lives Matter in America is an example of a large movement experiencing first-hand the difference linked to skin colour. Social inequality, corruption and mistreatment cause pressure. Pressure generates heat. If something gets hot enough, combustion follows. Laws change. Governments fall. Any mass protest, large-scale movement or war is the result of the pressure created by unbridled energy.

Disruptive leadership takes a lot of energy because for every leader who wants to make changes, there are a plethora of individuals or communities that will push back. Those who seek to protect the status quo are the majority. They try to dampen down and control anything that threatens their power, money or status. The bigger the desired change, the bigger the resistance. To return to the fire analogy, you could view those who seek to preserve the status quo as like ice. When water freezes, H_2O molecules line up uniformly like tightly packed soldiers on a parade ground. That's the status quo. It feels impenetrable. Rigid. Resistant. The status quo loves rules, systems, societal and cultural norms; a specific language, dress code and ways of conducting business. Throw in contracts, expectations, networks and procedures to protect what 'is' and all is well.

Disruptors are made of different stuff. They use their energy to think and act differently. They don't take no for an answer. When they hear, 'That is not how things are done around here,' they ask, 'Why not?' If something makes no sense, they call it out. Better still, they just go ahead and do it anyhow. (And guess what? Often, the naysayers are wrong.) Disruptors can be ignored, shunned and written about, and they often are at first, or they are perceived as nobodies, delusional or boisterous, arrogant up-starts. But disruptive leaders direct their energies to pressing on regardless. They don't stop because of what others say and think. They are willing to give everything to achieve their goal. They are bold and courageous. They are prepared to risk it all. To stand in their way is to ask for a fight. Disruptive leaders won't back down from adversity. They seek to kick conformity upside down and inside out.

The energy of a disruptive leader is infectious. If they direct it in the right way, others will align with the cause and willingly expend their energy to help a disruptive leader achieve their goal. There isn't much that's more exciting or fulfilling to be involved in. Done right, a disruptive leader and their followers (whether a team or organisation) will find true engagement and the effects will be felt far and wide.

The big question I asked myself was how I could help the leaders I work with to find this energy. For years, my focus had been on purpose. I'd had great success in helping individuals find their purpose, but that now needed to be combined with energy to achieve truly disruptive leadership. This is where the fire came in. As many may remember from their school days, there is a simple model for understanding the chemical reaction that must occur to create a fire. For a fire to ignite, there must be fuel, heat and oxygen. Remove one and you will end up like my barbequing friend: without the fire you want. Let's imagine the three elements working together to generate the energy for a disruptive fire:

- **Heat:** This is your energy in motion, starting with purpose and culminating in action.
- **Fuel:** The enthusiasm, excitement and engagement of the team. Fuel attracts the people, money and resources you need for your cause.
- **Oxygen:** Customers and consumers that sustain the combustion. This is your market and prevailing wind.

Combine these three elements and you will create fire. Energy driven by purpose, over a period, generates heat; add fuel and oxygen, and you have a disruptive fire:

$$\text{Heat (applied energy over time)} + \text{Fuel} + \text{Oxygen} = \text{Disruptive Fire}$$

The Covid-19 pandemic demonstrated what can happen when one of the elements is removed, or severely depleted. Many organisations were starved of oxygen (customers) thanks to the abrupt change in circumstance. Sadly, many did not have the resources or leadership to withstand this and keep their fire burning, let alone the company growing.

To grow the fire and, therefore, the level of disruption, a leader needs greater heat, more fuel and an increasing level of oxygen. Ultimately, it is the quality of your leadership that will define the kind and size of disruptive fire you become. Controlled fires achieve meaningful purpose through focus and discipline. In comparison, wildfires grow quickly but devastate everything in their path, and often die as quickly as they started.

I was sure I was onto something. My coaching experience showed me that it is important to break down concepts into bite-sized, easy-to-try tasks. This model was simple and eloquently illustrated all the elements required to generate the energy needed to pursue truly disruptive leadership. Everything fell into place.

The phone began to ring and work started coming in, even as I worked to perfect the new coaching model based on my fire analogy. Within six months, I had invoiced six figures. Numerous leading organisations were asking me to come and train dozens of their top leaders at a time. I was, I realised, a living and breathing example of my own leadership training. The moment I decided to prioritise my energy and time, I was able to apply it to begin generating (purposeful) heat. Once I added fuel and oxygen to my heat, a fire was lit. This time, though, I was sure to stay balanced. I knew from experience that I needed to focus my energy and time each day, or I would risk burnout.

A question I've been asked many times when faced with a difficult choice is, 'How should I decide what to do next?' For me, the answer is always the same: which choice most aligns with your purpose?

This was a question I had to ask myself once I met Katie Litchfield, founder of WeQual, an organisation seeking to drive gender equality at the top of the world's largest companies. Katie was a typical entrepreneurial disruptor. After running the *Financial Times* FT Forums for senior executives for several years, she was acutely aware of the lack of women at the top. She left the FT with a strong sense of purpose – she wanted to see equality at the top.[1] Despite having no money, no resources and no brand, she started WeQual. Six months later I was coaching her, as well as many of the incredible women she was finding as a result of the WeQual Awards (a robust assessment process which identifies and showcases women ready for a future C-suite role within globally listed companies). The more we did together, the more obvious it was that we could achieve so much more working together. Which begged a question for me – should I stop what I was doing, and join Katie?

Reminding myself that my purpose is to enable leaders to achieve meaningful purpose, here was an opportunity to do that on a global scale. Despite Covid-19 having just placed the entire world into lockdown, I was in.

Two of us, with a clear sense of purpose. We were starting a fire to challenge the status quo.

Not only is the analogy of fire a theoretical model, but it is also one I am living. Every day. I have known failure. Repeated failure. But that doesn't stop me. And it shouldn't stop you. With a strong enough purpose, you can overcome impossible odds. Apply your energy in the right way, and you increase heat. Attract the right fuel and get the needed oxygen; you will have your own disruptive fire.

In *Disruptive Leadership*, I have sought to document how you can apply what I've learned to your own leadership approach. In Part One, I will guide you on the best ways to get your fire started and on how to begin engaging your team so that they come with you on this journey of positive disruption. In Part Two, we will look at how to protect and maintain the fire, and in Part Three at how to fan the flames. I have also written a troubleshooting section, in Part Four, to conclude this book. One of the biggest dangers of disruptive leadership is getting complacent. This is where leaders relax and begin to bathe in their own success. Typically, success results in a new status quo. You then seek to protect what you have, rather than strive for greater change. From here, it is easy to leave the way open for another, more motivated disruptor.

There are numerous real-life examples throughout the book taken from interviews with some truly incredible business leaders from a wide range of sectors. I have asked them to reflect on their own path to disruption; their answers are inspiring and will go a long way towards helping you build and maintain your own fire. I have also included activities and exercises that will support you in beginning to put this newfound disruptive energy to work.

Disruptive Leadership will help you find your purpose and then apply energy to your disruptive fire.

Like anything new, it will take time to learn how to best apply it. Initially, it may be that perhaps just one or two individuals will warm to your cause. Maybe even imperceptibly at first. You'll secure a couple of meetings, or a handful of responses. Then, one or two prospects will become advocates. They'll reward you with small levels of engagement at first, but with continued application of energy you will start to thaw the market. As you grow your organisation or drive change, you will see a transformation taking place around you. Bit by bit, as you apply your energy, you will begin to win over important stakeholders. You will bring on board champions, sponsors, influencers, employee groups, management, suppliers and partners.

With the right proposition, and by combining heat, fuel and oxygen, you will challenge the status quo and question the way that things are done. As you draw people to your cause, disruption starts.

Disruptive Leadership is for those who want to make a difference. Those who seek to disrupt the way things are done. Those who, like a superhero, seek to bend every decision and apply every ounce of energy, every penny or cent, to achieve meaningful purpose.

Let's start a fire.

PART ONE
STARTING YOUR DISRUPTIVE FIRE

1
Heat

Picture the scene. It's hot. Very hot. That's usual for Saudi Arabia and, in particular, the Arabian Desert. It's especially the case in the region around the Sadara Chemical Company plant, the world's largest chemical complex ever built in a single phase (at a cost of more than $20 billion). The twenty-six large-scale manufacturing plants that make up the complex produce more than three million tonnes of petrochemical products every year. Today, a team from ABB is visiting one of the refineries. The global digital technology giant ABB, headquartered in Zurich, Switzerland, is the main automation contractor for this ambitious project, providing a range of software and hardware systems.

But there is a problem. It's not a problem to do with the complexity of the large contract. Everything has been going smoothly on that front. It is one of etiquette. The ABB team is led by Group Vice President Heather Cykoski. When companies in the Middle East do business with organisations from elsewhere, there are strict cultural rules about how interactions are negotiated. These rules govern how business partners greet one another, pursue conversations and manage the relationship. The potential sticking point here is that, in this part of the world, businesses are almost exclusively led by men. In fact, culture dictates that women are not even allowed in certain buildings. This, of course, presents a problem. Heather Cykoski is leading this project and she is there with her team. On arriving in the air-conditioned car at the guard gate, the security guard had no idea what to do when he saw a woman. Entry was not permitted. What would you do in this situation? The scenario is not unlike one any other would-be disruptors might face: a clear objective, with a major barrier. Critically, disruptors always find a way.

What did Heather do? Make a fuss? Brazenly head into the building anyway? She did neither of these things. Instead, she sent her (male) team in to conduct the meeting and communicated the plan with the team leading on her behalf. She supported them from the car via a two-way radio. Recounting the experience, she tells me:

'I understood and respected the culture, and that I could not go in because I was a woman. I was there to accomplish a goal and my best option was to ask my team to be the face of the meeting while I was the strategy behind them.

'I could have easily been frustrated and put myself in a situation where my actions weren't respectful. However, the ability to stay humble and appreciate cultures was paramount. Today, some of my best and closest relationships are with individuals that I interfaced with during that time. The entire project was an incredible opportunity to be a part of changing the land in the sands of Saudi.'

This behaviour is typical of Heather's approach. She's hugely competitive. In fact, her husband often jokes, 'Don't say to Heather that something can't be done, or she will run right through you on the way to doing it.' This desire to succeed means she won't always follow the obvious path. Even at school, her thought process was: where would she stand out as different? While in the youth organisation Distributive Education Clubs of America, she decided to ignore the marketing course she was encouraged to take and chose instead to study automotives because 'few other females did that'. She followed up by pursuing a career in industrial engineering, again a choice made by few women at the time. Her highly focused approach paid off and today she is leading ABB's efforts to accelerate new growth, managing relationships with customers worldwide.

Heather's strong sense of purpose has impacted the global sales team she has built. She doesn't always go for the obvious or safe choices. In one example, she hired a thirty-year-old woman with no engineering qualifications but a degree in language to lead ABB's efforts in the Middle East. Among the recruit's list of accomplishments was that she spoke fluent Chinese. Heather reasoned that since the Chinese were making huge investments in the region, a Chinese-speaking team member would help foster the much-needed trust-based relationships. In a short space of time, three significant contracts were signed, including for ABB's input into one of China's ubiquitous 'one belt, one road' projects.

This is one example of Heather's application of the 'coming to the edge' model brought in by ABB's chairman, Peter Voser, after his time at Shell. On this, she says:

> 'I'm looking for individuals that will bring
> something different to our network. There's too
> much following the status quo in this world,
> where people simply repeat the same thing over
> and over, even if it doesn't particularly work. My
> purpose is to find a new way of doing things.'

This new way of doing things has guided Heather and her organisation within ABB, driving $2 billion per annum sales within six years. It's fair to say her approach works.

Before you assume that disruptors like Heather must be egocentric, consider that during our research we dubbed Heather the 'Queen of Hearts'. Her mother's constant question to her has always been, 'Are you being kind?' If you ever have the privilege of meeting Heather, you will know the answer.

Understand yourself

All disruptive leadership begins with purpose. We decide what difference we want to make (what it is we feel most enthusiastic or dissatisfied about) and start to expend energy to bring about the change we desire. This brings us up against the status quo, the sole purpose of which is to stop us making a difference. In the corporate world, that might be other businesses that don't want you to take their market share, customers who may not be sufficiently convinced to give you their money or an internal culture that resists necessary transformation. If you want to change the status quo, you need to generate heat – this means that, like Heather, you need to be passionate about driving change.

The disruptive fire model always begins with purpose. You can't be a disruptive leader if you are not fully behind the disruption you want to see. Whenever I start working with a leader, I always begin by asking the same question:

'What do you want to do with your life?'

It's a question I've asked thousands of times, and now that you are at the beginning of this process, I am asking you. I am fairly confident you will give me the same answer as almost everyone else. Depending on what stage you're at in your life and career, you will either tell me that you want a good job, a nice house, a loving partner, a happy family and career success, or that you want to make a difference. These are all common desires; they're the answers I most frequently hear, and rightly so. But I would press you to go deeper. Who are you? What do you truly value? What is it about you that makes you unique? What gets you excited?

REFLECTIVE EXERCISE: What's your purpose?

Consider the following:

- When you reach the end of your life, what is it you want to have achieved? Try to write your own 500-word obituary. What would you like your obituary to say?
- What would you like to be said in a speech at your retirement party? If a major newspaper or magazine wrote an article about your career, what would the piece say? Start with some bullet points, give it some thinking time, and write your own article.

This might be the first time you've given this serious consideration, in which case start more generically and consider the types of things that matter most to you. If right now the whole-life view is too long for you, take a shorter-term perspective. Figure out what three key accomplishments you want to be able to write on your CV/resume in, say, three years' time.

If you've not taken the time to properly think through the answer to the question of what you want to do with your life, being asked about your purpose is tough. Some people think they are too busy to think about such things. If this is you, I would argue that you are filling your life with the wrong things. It is easy to be 'busy'. It provides a constant dopamine hit. You're busy, therefore you are important. Think about it a different way. Is your perpetual need to keep (or at least appear) busy simply a way of trying to meet some deep internal need for self-worth through seeking the approval of others? The problem is, by only doing what you believe other people want you to do, you don't give yourself the time and space to look internally. You're not considering what *you* want. The result is often a reactive life where you allow others to call the shots. 'Go here.' 'Do this.' 'Wait.' 'Don't take the risk.'

Just for a moment, ignore the demands of daily living that can so easily eat up all of our attention. Forget about survival, about impressing others or attaining the next goal. All of these things crowd out our deepest need: to make a difference. Life is short. If we are not proactive in being purposeful with our lives, our final days will be full of regret. I'll ask again:

What do you *really* want to do with your life?

It has taken me years of reflection and distillation to be able to state my professional purpose in a single sentence: enabling leaders to achieve meaningful purpose. Since being a small child I've sought to help others achieve their purpose, and now have the immense joy of working with incredible leaders and the organisations they run. This sense of purpose runs through me like the letters through a stick of rock (candy). If you cut me open, that is what I will bleed.

If you don't know what you stand for, neither will anyone else.

Ultimately, your answer to the above question will typically be a variation on one word: *impact*.

Everybody wants to make a difference. We all want to have a purpose. Asking yourself these questions will help you understand more about yours. True impact starts with understanding what we are about as leaders. What is the change we desire to see? We all have a purpose and, once we begin the pursuit of that purpose, we can have a tremendous positive impact. I am constantly astounded, exhilarated, even humbled, when those I coach share their deepest desires. Call me an optimist, but I believe that with the right environment each of us can achieve our purpose and leave the world a better place.

Once you have articulated your purpose and the difference you want to make, you will need to find the energy to fight the inevitable resistance you will find along the way. The dissatisfaction you feel about your business' place in the market, the state of the world or a certain situation can provide the initial heat, but to start the fire you need more. Feel angry about difference all you like, but it is only when you do something about your dissatisfaction that disruption can start to take place.

What does 'doing something' look like? Think back to any time in the past when you effected change of some kind. Would any of the following describe what you did?

Questioning	Challenging	Leaving
Shouting	Walking/running	Writing
Screaming	Fighting	Pushing
Investing	Denying	Allowing
Releasing	Resisting	Joining
Campaigning	Championing	Starting

Doing something is energy in motion, and energy in motion generates heat. It's a law of the universe. It's the same principle as rubbing your hands to warm them on a cold day, or turning on a kettle, which causes an electrical current to heat an element to boil water.

REFLECTIVE EXERCISE: What's driving you?

Reflect on the following questions:

- Who is in control of your life and choices?
- What are the drivers in your life that are shaping your future?
- What is it you want?

Difference drives energy

Bob was appointed CEO after a protracted process. On his first day he chose to sit in reception and watch what happened while his identity was still unknown.

The décor was dated. Lots of employees sauntered in late. The receptionist chewed gum as she answered the phone. Visitors were kept waiting. Feeling a little disconcerted, he began to move around the corridors. There he saw people laughing, joking and gossiping while they drank coffee. Little work seemed to be being done. When Bob peered into the meeting rooms, they were untidy and mostly empty. Confidential customer information was left out on desks. As he walked the floors, he heard people complaining about poor IT. After two hours, he'd seen enough.

In the scientific world, difference is what creates energy flow. Thermodynamics teaches us that the difference between two temperatures results in what we experience as heat. Heat will always 'flow' from hot to cold – a hot radiator will heat a cold room. In a similar way, electricity flows between positive and negative. The bigger the difference, the greater the flow of energy required.

We rely on difference in every aspect of our lives. The difference between feeling hungry or full causes us to eat. The difference between our current and ideal weight causes us to exercise. Think about the last time you had an argument or got upset. It was almost certainly due to a difference in opinion or expectations. The result was a range of emotions and feelings that were expressed in some way. Without difference, there is no transfer of energy. The more we perceive difference, the more energy is released to do something about it.

Bob experienced difference. There was a gulf between what he expected at his new company, and what he saw. The more he saw, the more his blood boiled. The hotter he got, the more he wanted to change what he saw. Now imagine Bob's first weeks in charge. His highly energised state will vibrate and collide with others. Some will welcome it, while others will feel threatened. It might take time, but one thing is for sure: as his heat energy flows into the business, it will impact those around him and Bob will begin to disrupt the status quo.

Where or when do you feel like Bob? What is it you perceive, experience or are impacted by that you want to change? I guarantee that if you feel it strongly enough, you will want to act. Poor customer service? Plastics in our oceans? Sustainability within the supply chain? Lack of effective strategy? Equal opportunities for all? Poor medical care? Child safety? It is within your power to use that fiery heat of your disappointment or frustration to solve the problems you see. Each week provides us with hundreds of opportunities to act to challenge the status quo.

Difference makes us feel uncomfortable. It asks something of us. Are we prepared to do something about it? If we feel it strongly enough, we act. We ask difficult questions. We are prepared to collide with others and create conflict. Disagreement provides the spark of new ideas. People think about ways to improve, innovate and disrupt.

Disruptive leaders are driven by their desire to bridge difference.

REFLECTIVE EXERCISE: Where's your difference?

Answer the following questions:

- Where do you see a difference that you can't shake off? What does different look like for you?
- What captures your attention and energy, with a desire to change it? What do you want to do about it?

If you are unclear, take some time to reflect. The clearer you are, the easier your life choices will be, and the more intentional your focus and impact.

How much heat is needed?

As a rule, the larger the scale of disruption you seek, the more difficult it will be to ignite change in your chosen market. Likewise, the more resistant (cold) your target market is to your desired change, the more heat you will need.

To understand why, consider the humble battery. Its energy flows from the plus to the minus terminal. It is a hard and fast rule that the bigger the difference between the plus and minus, the more energy is required to overcome it. If, say, you ran a small hairdressing salon and wanted to change the terms of employment of one or two employees, that would be a lot easier than trying to alter working conditions in a heavily unionised national rail company. It would take a lot of energy to bridge that gap. After all, the moment you expend force in one direction, there is an equal and opposite force in the other direction. The bigger the force, the bigger the resistance.

As Steve Cahillane, who joined the Kellogg Company as CEO in 2017, attests, the status quo can be a powerful foe when there is a large, and often influential, cohort who seem to have a vested interest in keeping things as they are, or at least not changing anything a great deal. In a heritage business like this US-based multinational food manufacturer with a more than hundred-year history behind it, there is not much appetite for big shifts in strategy. As Steve describes to me:

'In my first sixty days in the business, I spent my whole time on the road, complete with old-school yellow notepads, which I completely filled with notes. I asked everyone, "What is it going to take to grow this business again?" What came through was a very clear message that we had spent too many years focused on cutting costs in the organisation and introducing zero-based budgeting. These things aren't bad things and they were done very, very well. The hypothesis I developed was: if we put in as much effort in the future, and exert as much discipline into growing the business as we have in reducing costs, we can turn it around. We can turn our top line back to growth.

'When you pivot and change the mindset to focus on growth, there is a lot that is out of your control. There's also a lot that stands in your way: competitors, customers, advertising agencies, everyone. There were very few, if any, in the analyst community that thought we could grow. Meanwhile, the business press was focused on the next shiny object. They'd look at industries like ours and say there is nothing interesting in packaged food. They'd say the focus is all on fresh foods that can be grown in our gardens. While that was true, you only needed to take one look at our snacking business – it was on fire.'

Disrupting the status quo takes some serious energy and resources, as Steve explains. Each of Kellogg's brands needed some 'innovation dollars' put behind it. But what really shifted the dial was getting the internal resources behind the strategy.

'The challenge was making sure everyone on the team and the board of directors believed in it. There was a fair bit of movement in the leadership ranks early on because if you don't believe, won't at least give the strategy a chance, or aren't 100% committed, then you have to move on. Even then, there were still some sceptics, but it was my job to keep pushing. I needed to get the team's hearts engaged. I couldn't just be a cheerleader for what I wanted to do. While a lot comes from the CEO, I don't make all the decisions, or come up with the best ideas. I needed to create the type of environment and processes that drove the search for ideas. I had to align my team towards this belief, and then all the other stakeholders.

'One of our runaway successes was a baked snack brand called Cheez-It. I looked at it and said, "Boy, this brand is just a gem. What have we been doing? We haven't been innovating enough." The team got innovating and came up with a new platform called Grooves, which was a runaway success. We couldn't make enough. Every good innovation we put behind Cheez-It since has been a home run for us. It started in the USA, then we launched it in Canada and Brazil, and Europe will be next. We are going to take that brand global.

'We are constantly challenging our thinking with each brand. That's not to say we rip it all up and start again. We just look at what is working and what isn't and what is required for us to be successful in the future.'

As Steve found, disrupting the status quo takes a large amount of energy to generate the necessary heat. It requires clarity of direction and a determination to overcome what stands in your way. This is not an easy path, and it's not for the faint-hearted.

Your own heat will come from the difference you seek, which will drive your action accordingly. Your personal drive is what will bridge that difference.

Consider, as an example, these vision statements:

- 'A just world without poverty'

- 'The world's most loved, most flown and most profitable airline'

- 'A world without Alzheimer's'

However improbable, implausible or impossible these goals, considerable energy is required in the pursuit of them. It is certainly not possible to alleviate poverty or cure an illness with half-hearted measures. We cannot transform a business with mere desire.

Fire is unpredictable. The amount of heat you will need to start your disruptive fire will depend on many variables. As anyone who hails from the business world will attest, some projects require an inordinate amount of energy to get started, while others take very little. Once started, some successfully continue with minimal effort, and others demand everything you have, and more. Those who run successful projects effortlessly will often claim it is a result of their own talent, but it is not always as simple as that as the following three scenarios illustrate.

So how does a fire start?

Inspiring early adopters – the flashpoint

In fire terms, the flashpoint is the lowest temperature at which a material will ignite when a source of ignition is supplied, whether that's a match to a barbeque or an electric spark in a gas oven. This scenario is similar to a startup, or an established business entering a new market. As a disruptive leader, you are the ignition source. Your applied energy provides the required heat. Without you, there is no fire. No change. Get it right and you will inspire a trickle of the most adventurous and attract them to your cause. These will be your first customers/backers/supporters. The trick is to then build upon this small fire.

Any disruptive product requires significant behavioural change. The bell curve of the potential market response is eloquently described in Geoffrey Moore's book *Crossing the Chasm*.[2] To begin with, small numbers of innovators will buy in, followed by early adopters. These are the type of people who always want to be the first to try new things and are open to risk. The challenge lies in the next (larger) group on the bell curve, the early majority, who have an entirely different mindset. They are far more pragmatic and risk-averse. They consistently buy from well-known brands because it is safe to do so. It is this majority that you need to win over to gain real traction and become a dominant player. The messages that will get this next group on board will be different.

Moore suggests picking a niche to overcome the chasm and gain early majority customers, slowly building up the heat. Become known as an expert with a strong claim, regardless of the quirkiness of the niche. For example, you might launch the 'world's best' wild boar steak knife. Or the best-performing and most diverse team in the Mid-West. Or the only online meeting place for those studying medicine in the North West. Once you've succeeded and gained customer references, social credibility and a reputation, you can call yourself a market leader. Keep adding more niches until you reach a critical mass. You will now have a trusted brand and increasing numbers will buy from you.

Right place, right time – spontaneous combustion

Spontaneous combustion, or auto ignition, is the temperature at which a material will 'burst' into flames. Here, there is no external ignition, and the fire will continue to burn until the material is spent. Mass movements self-ignite without formal leaders, rage across a landscape, then often burn out. Others have a lasting impact. The fall of the Berlin Wall is a good example of auto ignition. A disenfranchised, under-pressure population spontaneously combusted. There was no single leader. To the outsider, it seemed to come from nowhere.

Within a business setting, we can see this spontaneous combustion in products that, completely unexpectedly, sell like wildfire for no apparent reason. They become the 'in' thing almost overnight.

Over the years, there have been numerous crazes that lift off, then die, from loom band elastic bracelets to Rubik's Cubes. (Spontaneous combustion can also cause unwanted disruption – for example, if employees decide they've had enough of working overtime to produce plastic toys and walk out on strike.)

A product going viral is every marketeer's dream, yet it is difficult to engineer. Tapping into a large group of people's current thinking or pressure points is difficult. Even if you are blessed to be in the right place at the right time, there are no guarantees as to how long it will last. Rest assured, it won't be long before disruption will knock at your door and the crowd will move on to the next craze. Warren Buffet often talks about the rise and fall of brands and relates the phenomenon closely to reputation.[3] An organisation that has a good reputation is more likely to stand the test of time and keep its product in the mainstream than one that has become an overnight success. It's the same reason why someone would buy a watch for £5,000 when there are copies available for £50. A good reputation does not come about by accident. It requires a consistent focus on values and purpose. Effort and money need to be expended on putting the customer first, ensuring quality and consistency – plus a whole lot of marketing.

Momentum – fire point

The fire point is the lowest temperature at which a material will keep burning on its own. For example, once a piece of paper has been lit, it no longer requires the match. This is the moment that a change, or offering, 'catches' – as the disruptor, you are likely to feel elated. Now there is momentum. The conditions have changed and the market is responding positively. It has become mainstream. The change has been adopted and becomes the new status quo. Watch out, though, as new disruptors will seek to disrupt you.

When you look at these scenarios, it is easy to say there is an element of luck involved, particularly in the case of spontaneous combustion. In each instance, though, however easy the ignition, keeping the fire burning is the challenge. That is where you need to bring your heat to bear. Focus on the difference you seek to bridge. Let it burn within you. Let nothing take you off course. Heat causes discomfort. If you keep applying it over time, it forces others to make a decision: join you, or fight. When enough of them join, you will have momentum.

REFLECTIVE EXERCISE: Quantify your difference

Take a few minutes to answer the following questions:

- What is the core difference you want to make? Specify it as clearly as you can.
- How strongly do you feel about it?
- Is it a choice, or do you feel compelled to act?
- What is a likely timescale?
- How much energy will be needed to achieve it?

2
But I'm No One Special

Regardless of how you feel about yourself, the moment you gain the title 'manager', 'executive' or 'boss', everything changes. Even with a direct report of just one, you gain the power to answer questions such as, 'Can I take a day off? Can I take my lunch hour early? What should I work on next? Can I move my desk? Can I have a tattoo? Is this good work? Can I have a pay rise? Can I go for a promotion?'

Leaders aren't superheroes

There is often a perception that leaders are a super-human breed. That those in leadership have superpowers. They don't feel as we mere mortals do. They think strategically, have high levels of emotional intelligence, stay calm in a crisis and have unparalleled levels of resilience. Yet in reality, any leader or manager is as human as you and I. They struggle with prioritisation, dread difficult conversations, work long hours, battle with exhaustion, have challenges at home and often wonder whether they are on the right path. I say this to encourage you. Disruptive leaders are not superheroes; what they are, is united in their drive to make a difference. This, aligned with a set of lived values, is what will make your fire succeed where others will fail.

Srimathi Shivashankar was one of the leaders I spoke to who highlighted how much her personal life and past have impacted her purpose and approach to her career. Srimathi is the corporate VP at HCL Technologies, an Indian multinational that is now the world's number three in IT services and a pioneer in infrastructure management serving Fortune 500 and Global 2000 companies.

Srimathi was born in a small village in the district of Ariyalur, Tamil Nadu, India. From an early age, she sensed that learning to speak English would help her become more assertive, after feeling acutely embarrassed whenever her English-speaking cousins visited. While she struggled with learning the language, particularly in the context of subjects like science and maths, one teacher took an interest in her progress and would stay back after school to help her. The efforts of Srimathi and her teacher paid off. She started her career in IT, first as a coder and later selling industrial computers (an unusual and challenging choice for a woman in India) and then into a corporate role where she rose to become the first diversity officer in India, followed by the first sustainability officer. But despite her professional training and experience, it is her personal life that has done the most to shape her purpose.

Srimathi has two children, a son and a daughter, and her son was born with multiple disabilities. On finding out about her son's issues, she asked her mother, 'Why me?' Her mother replied, 'Why not you?' This response helped shape Srimathi into the amazing disruptive leader she is today.

She has learned a lot from her son, she tells me. In particular, she recalls the pivotal moment when she and her husband had returned home from the hospital, having just learned that their now teenage son had lost sight in his one remaining eye:

'As we stood there discussing whether I should give up work, my son left his bedroom, went to the bathroom and returned to his room – all unaided. In that moment, I realised how much I had underestimated his potential. He taught me how to appreciate true potential through the way he deals with things and manages himself. This has become a central philosophy of mine when we think of our employees. If we are not careful, we limit what our people can do. Yet as my son taught me, people can do so much more if they are given the opportunity.

'He also taught me that, as a leader, I may
have setbacks, but the only choice is to move
forward. You don't wait for choices to appear;
you move on by making your own way.'

Srimathi's experiences fuelled her interest in diversity
from the outset of her career (she was India's first chief
diversity officer at Infosys back in 2006). On moving
to HCL Technologies, she set about shifting their culture to be more diverse and inclusive – putting people
at the heart of the company. She was responsible for
strategising and operationalising new HCL delivery
centres through the New Vistas programme designed
to establish innovation and delivery centres in emerging Tier 2 cities around the world. She took the
ground-breaking approach of going where the talent
was, with a focus on women, rather than expecting
the talent to come to them.

Srimathi created 20,000 new roles across the
globe and women now make up about 30% of HCL's
employees. It's a strategy she is fully behind because
she knows it will make the whole business stronger.
Her people-first approach allowed her to successfully
move on to lead strategy for large-scale transformation programmes, and she has been taking on large
P&L roles since 2015. She tells me:

'An organisation is made by the people,
for the people. If you develop a diverse
workplace, where people are very
different and can bring in their own ideas

to help you shape your purpose, then it creates a collective accountability. This is why I have been successful in all my transformation programmes.'

As we chatted about her career, I suggested that culture change and transformation is only possible when executives take the lead. She disagreed...

'Harnessing the power of the workforce is often misunderstood. People talk about the "ripple effect" where the more senior you are, and the better your performance, the greater the impact on the team as the impact ripples through it. In reality, the ripple effect is not about taking the leader's vision forward. The ripple effect is actually about collaboration, about getting people to come together and enabling them to give constructive feedback, or even to critique the strategy of a leader. In my view, the best ripple effect happens in adversity, when people are allowed to critique the actions of a leader. Their choice of words makes you question what you are doing. When you have a workplace where people are very different, with a range of views and backgrounds, that is even more powerful.'

No wonder Srimathi was named as one of the Top 25 Women Leaders in Consulting for 2022 and 2023 by *The Consulting Report*.[4]

The confidence to disrupt

Srimathi is an experienced and confident leader, but not all leaders have these qualities. Many leaders struggle with low levels of confidence. There's even a name for it: imposter syndrome. 'How did I get here?' these leaders ask themselves. 'When will I be found out?'

It's more common than you might think. I've lost count of the number of times leaders have confided that they live with a permanent sense of dread that they are about to be 'found out'. They feel like imposters, their blood full of adrenaline, constantly trying to prove themselves. It is often comforting to realise you are not alone in feeling like this. In fact, well over half of those we coach struggle with confidence. Often in these cases, I remind leaders that courage matters more than confidence. After all, confidence is not a predictor of success. Many strong and highly successful leaders have scored very low on confidence assessments, but it is their courage that drives their outstanding results. They are doing the right thing *despite* their fear and uncertainty.

What can be surprising to these leaders is how others perceive them. In fact, they often describe their peers (other leaders) in glowing and inspirational terms – when I know those same leaders sometimes feel crippled by imposter syndrome. Aside from demonstrating that often our perception of ourselves is off (and this is where feedback and coaching really help), it also highlights that we are not aware of the impact we have on others.

By the time we find ourselves in a senior position, we set the tone for everyone, regardless of our confidence. A leader defines the who, what, where, how and why. And not just on the big things. If you like a document to be presented in a certain way, woe betide anyone who doesn't comply. If you want certain words to be used, used they must be. If you dress smartly, there will be an expectation that your team dress smartly too. If you do or don't swear, your team will follow your lead. If you get in early, answer emails at the weekend and check Slack at midnight, there will be pressure to do the same. Get the idea?

Followers follow. Why? Because leaders have power. If you understand your purpose and how your organisation needs to change in order to fulfil that purpose, you ensure that those who follow you, and those you influence, are caught up in something meaningful, regardless of personal levels of confidence. The bigger the difference you feel, the more energy you have and the more heat you generate. Doesn't it make sense that the person leading the change and culture of your organisation is the person looking at you in the mirror?

REFLECTIVE EXERCISE: Your influence

Answer the following questions:

- Despite how you might feel about your own strengths and weaknesses, what level of power and influence do you have over those you lead?
- How can you increase your influence to drive the change you seek?

If you have answered that your power and influence are small, start where you are. Take time out to redefine *why* you are in the role you are.

There is no time for half-heartedness. Heat is uncompromising. The higher the heat, the higher the chance of disruption. Only high heat sets fire to things to achieve disruption.

Heat manifests itself in every action you take. It's in the language you use: urgent, now, tomorrow. It's in the way you make decisions: quickly, decisively. It's in the things you won't tolerate: endless meetings, slipping deadlines. It's in the diversity and strength of the team you build around you. If passivity rules and you are going with the flow, that is low energy. You need to refocus on your difference. Go back to your purpose. Is what currently fills your calendar helping you achieve it? If not, something needs to change.

Disruptors don't wait. They act. Because the difference demands it. If you know your purpose and are inspired by difference, act now. As a leader, you are in a position to change things. Start applying that heat today.

REFLECTIVE EXERCISE: Your ability to disrupt

What is it you want to disrupt? What is the difference you want to see?

Answer the following questions and rate yourself on a scale of 0 to 100 (0 is low, 100 is high):

- I feel uniquely gifted to bring about this change.
- How disruptive is the change?
- Who or what stands in your way? How strong is the resistance?
- How much energy is needed to overcome the resistance?
- How strongly do you feel about the difference you want to make?
- How energised do you feel about the desired change?

If you scored yourself lower than you'd like on the uniquely gifted question – welcome to the club. Feel and channel the difference strongly enough, and no one will be able to stand in your way.

If you scored lower on the energy and feeling scales – don't worry; you're not alone. You are an amazing human being who is either in the wrong place, or just exhausted. I will speak more about energy and time (including how to get more of them) later in the book.

A final point to reflect on: what has stood out or surprised you in this chapter?

3
Fuel

Forget about the cliché of the swaggering leader who can do no wrong. We all have strengths and weaknesses, however committed we are to our purpose and driving our organisation forward to achieve our goals. We are, after all, human. Plus, if the disruptive ambition is substantial, we'd be a fool to try to go it alone. This means we need resources. Resources are the fuel that help our fire burn. Fuel is the material full of potential energy. In our case, the fuel is primarily made up of people and cash.[5] If you don't have fuel, you are simply a hothead with a big idea. With fuel, you have the opportunity to be a fire starter.

Let's start with people.

People

People are an amazing type of fuel. Being part of a disruptive movement energises everyone involved. Engagement levels are off the charts. This in turn gives you a competitive advantage, a greater source of innovation and growing revenues. As momentum builds, a belief takes hold that the impossible is possible. Yes, it can be hard work, but there is joy and fulfilment too. There is no more exciting place to be than working alongside others with a vision to achieve.

When a leader's passion inspires others, it's like playing an E note on a piano and hearing the guitar in the same room start to resonate (a guitar has two E strings). The clearer a leader is about their purpose and the more energy they expend in seeking to fulfil it, the more attracted like-minded people will be to the cause. Birds of a feather flock together.

If you want to be truly disruptive, it is imperative that you vibrate clearly. If you sound a D#, only badly tuned guitars will respond. Many leaders, if asked, would say they were clear about their purpose. Yet, according to Gallup, only 22% of employees strongly agree that their leaders have a clear direction.[6] That means around eight out of ten leaders reading this book are either not clear about their purpose or are not living it. If either of these apply to you, it will be costing you dearly. If no one understands what they are there for, you'll see lower engagement, revenues and profits. Lack of urgency results in inefficiency, procrastination, prevarication and paralysing conflict. Employees will feel frustrated and confused, and the best ones will leave. After all, 70% of the variance in team engagement is determined solely by the manager.[7]

It is imperative that leaders ensure their purpose is clear, compelling and understood by all. In the previous chapter, you articulated your purpose. This was not a one-off exercise, to be quietly forgotten about as you get on with the day job. That purpose should be central to everything you do. As I've already said, mine is to enable leaders to achieve meaningful purpose. My own purpose underpins everything I do – and so should yours.

As well as repeating your purpose at every given opportunity, every decision must be made in line with it. Every penny spent, every hiring decision, every marketing campaign, every aspect of research and development, every training programme, every engagement with customers, every project is embarked on with that purpose in mind. Get it right and you will experience a sustained increase in temperature.

A disruptive leader must ensure their vision is compelling and urgent. Shout it from the rooftops. Vibrate with it. Loud and clear. When you have urgency, everyone will prioritise. Spend will be targeted. Executives will be held to account. You will create a culture of 'us' not 'I'. Vanity projects will be abandoned. Every employee will understand why they are employed. Every department, every decision, every meeting, every conversation, every penny and every breath will be directed towards achieving that purpose. Being part of something with a powerful, uniting vision is life-giving, purpose-inducing and energy-releasing.

REFLECTIVE EXERCISE: Review your purpose

Revisit your personal purpose – can you write it in a single sentence? If you are still not clear, start more generically and speak to the types of things that matter the most to you.

Once you have it clear, tell everyone you know and work with.

Enthuse, excite, engage

A vet's life is a stressful one. They study for years, are often paid poorly and work long hours. Many of those hours are at unsociable times and, if they are not in the surgery, vets are frequently on call. They also work with a range of animals, whereas doctors deal with only one type of mammal. Even with this undoubted pressure, and despite an obvious sense of purpose (a desire to help animals), you might be shocked to learn that veterinarians are twice as likely to die by suicide as doctors or dentists, and up to six times more likely than the general population.[8] An estimated 50% of vets are considering leaving their practice and veterinary hospitals experience turnover twice that of other industries.[9]

This is clearly an industry ripe for urgent disruption, which is exactly what Tim Harrison, the managing director of White Cross Vets, identified. I first became aware of this company when I met two of its team at an event. The two young vets talked enthusiastically about their employer, highlighting how the company had looked after them during times of crisis, as well as the multiple benefits they received. I was intrigued – since I was aware of the challenges vet businesses faced – and keen to meet the White Cross Vets MD who had made this happen. I was delighted when I subsequently discovered that I would be sharing the stage with Tim at a conference on wellbeing. By this stage, his business had grown from one to nineteen practices across England. To say that Tim was passionate about employee engagement was an understatement. Here are just some of the employee benefits White Cross Vets had introduced:

- Private healthcare
- Twenty-four-hour counselling
- 8% contributory pension
- Five weeks' paid holiday
- No out-of-hours work
- Discounts for family and friends
- Extra day's holiday on birthday plus personalised gift
- Five days' CPD with funding

- Four days' paternity leave

- £100 towards annual gym costs

- £50 towards a Fitbit

- £500 gift on birth of first baby

Tim's purpose was to build a company where employees wanted to give their energy, while also being protected from burnout. He told me:

> 'Our level of engagement through our culture was indeed industry-leading, but it was equally due to the respect we gave individuals and the support we provided when they needed it. It was as much the everyday behaviour towards our team that led to the culture experience we had, not just the benefits and things that were given.'

Managers were supportive and caring and would always go the extra mile for their employees. Unsurprisingly, the employees responded in kind. White Cross Vets became a profitable business and was able to expand, establishing new practices through positive cash flow. The customers loved the organisation too and it had a reputation for outstanding levels of customer care. Numerous awards were forthcoming, including six consecutive years of being listed in *The Sunday Times* Best Small Companies to Work For (2013–2018), as well as multiple other business awards across the UK and Europe. In May 2018, White Cross

Vets was sold to Independent Vet Care (IVC) at a multiplier previously unheard of in the industry.

Contrast this with a management team I worked with, which I won't name for reasons that will become obvious. Trust had completely broken down in Company X; fear ruled and eggshells adorned the floor. It was apparent to even the most casual observer that more effort was being expended in managing personal anxiety and stress among multiple team members than in achieving objectives. The performance of this company was appalling.

This second scenario is depressingly common. According to Gallup, only 15% of global employees are engaged.[10] That is staggering. Imagine getting in your car to drive home one evening but only being able to extract 15% of its performance. You wouldn't even be able to see the road properly because you'd only have 15% of the lights. And what does this lack of engagement cost? An estimated $7 trillion in lost productivity.

Employee engagement is a buzzword much loved by HR, and for good reason. Yet how many people really understand what this means? It's more than job satisfaction, discretionary effort, job involvement or commitment, though all of these are relevant. For true engagement you need to add persistence, focused energy, motivation, adaptability, positivity, task completion and achievement. All these things are directed towards achieving purpose. Each member of the team brings their all, adding their own fuel to the fire. Every individual has a particular mix of potential and kinetic energy. Effort in action is the kinetic part. The most successful organisations engage their people in such a way as to release the most amount of potential energy possible, while protecting against burnout.

Even small movements in this direction can have astonishing results. According to a Kenexa study across twenty-seven countries, a 1% increase in employee engagement was linked to a 4.8% increase in GDP.[11] Increased engagement not only boosts revenues, but also profitability, customer service, innovation and wellbeing, and reduces staff absences. Get it right and you can increase discretionary effort by 57%.[12] That's equivalent to having 1.5 times the number of people working for you, for the same cost. It's hardly surprising that highly engaged workforces outperform their peers by 147% in earnings per share.[13]

A myriad of consulting firms are paid billions of dollars every year to help firms increase engagement. Yet engagement levels remain stubbornly consistent. Investing in an 'engagement programme' is not enough. Good engagement comes from good leadership. As leaders, we have a responsibility to ensure that our people's expenditure of energy is worthwhile and not wasted.

As a starting point, look at any engagement activities you've done to date. Ask yourself honestly, was your engagement survey just a tick-box exercise? Did the board review the results? Were any suggested improvement plans that came out of it championed at the highest levels? When absences increase and retention decreases, is there a tendency to see it as 'normal'? If you've ever been challenged about this, do you find yourself saying, 'But you don't understand our sector – we are unique'? Rubbish. The veterinary industry most likely considers itself unique, yet we've already seen how Tim Harrison bucked the trend. It doesn't take long to obliterate the 'but we're different' argument. As Tim Harrison clearly demonstrated, treating the team well is key to engagement. Their behaviours, as well as White Cross Vets' substantial list of employee benefits, went a long way towards making a stressful working environment a better place to be.

Something else that is crucial to engagement is to treat your team as individuals. While a disruptive leader has a clear sense of their purpose, every effort must be made to align that with each person's own sense of purpose.

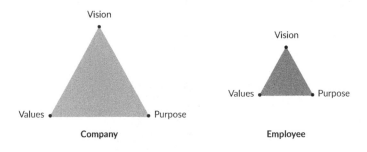

What a disengaged employee looks like

In the image above, we see the company, where the leaders are clear on what they want to do. They've mapped out their purpose, values and vision and are on their way to changing the part of the world they feel destined to change. A long way to one side is an employee, who has a completely different sense of purpose. They have their own vision for their life and career and live by an entirely different set of values. The only reason they are working at the company is because they are being paid to do so. If they got a better offer at an organisation that more closely reflected their purpose, values and vision, they'd be off like a shot. Are they engaged with the company? Not even close.

For full engagement, your goal as a disruptive leader is to align people's personal sense of purpose with the organisational purpose – see the figure below. If a team member is interested in climate change, bring them into a project related to that and they will be significantly more likely to do everything they can to make it a success. They will give it their energy and time and be much more engaged.

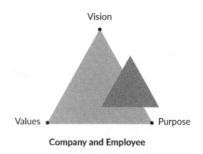

What an engaged employee looks like

All those wonderful people on your team are full of energy, which is potential fuel for your cause. It is your responsibility as a leader to make sure that energy is not wasted. Leave them to become disengaged and there will be a cost. Their resistance to your purpose will drain fuel from the company. Any resisters will make others uncomfortable too – doing nothing about employee engagement is not an option.

Ensuring a team is engaged doesn't always happen naturally; it takes time and attention to detail from managers. This was a lesson learned by Jasi Halai, the chief operating officer of the FTSE 50 international private equity and infrastructure investor, 3i. Jasi admits that, early in her career when she first began leading teams and projects, she received feedback that she needed to slow down and let others do the thinking too. She tells me:

'It is my style to work at a fast pace and try to anticipate what may occur further down the track, which means I can unintentionally lead the way. This could sometimes make others feel they were not heard, or that they simply had to follow what I had set out. I realised that to arrive at the best solution and get the most out of my team, I needed to slow down and give the team time to identify pitfalls and solutions and then nurture and guide them to delivery.'

Initially, Jasi found this challenging. But over time she realised that bringing the team alongside her was essential, especially when collaborating on larger international projects. Taking input from teams in different countries was essential in reaching the best solution and ensuring the wider team was on board with both the process and outcome. Today, she credits her success to the people-orientated approach she has taken at 3i.

'The type of organisation we are means we attract hugely talented people. Everyone has something to contribute, and it is up to me to get the most out of them.'

To Jasi, there are two key elements to achieving this ideal: shared purpose and trust.

'I'm a great believer in Karma; what goes around comes around. These are values that I've grown up with and which I aim to follow in both my personal and professional life. At work, I want to help build sustainable businesses that will grow and be successful for the right reasons. When spending company money, I always ask myself, would I spend or invest my own money like this? This approach is something that I have instilled in my team. Likewise, if I work with an organisation, I want to know, how are we making sure we are getting value for money? Have we done all the checks we would do if we were spending our own money? I expect the same discipline whether we are spending £99 or £99 million.'

To achieve this ideal, Jasi says her relationship with her team is built on trust.

'The critical part of earning trust is making sure you are listening. When you are working in a high-achieving environment, it's easy to give orders, but not as straightforward to listen. But if you pause and create a safe space, people will come and tell you what is making them uncomfortable; they will offer solutions to problems that they come across and they will feel empowered to suggest alternative ways of dealing with issues and situations.

'Part of creating that safe space is making it clear that mistakes are OK. Everyone comes to work with good intentions, however at times things can go wrong. My approach is to support the team and look at solutions, how can we move to a glass half-full mindset rather than glass half-empty? We learn the most from mistakes, or from projects that initially may not seem exciting or are extremely difficult to deliver. If there are no mistakes, we are neither learning nor growing. Some sleepless nights are helpful in pushing ourselves to do more.

'When a team is motivated, understands the bigger picture and has the space to do what is expected of them, the results are always better. Together we can achieve great things, to lift yourself you have to help lift others. This, in turn, creates a shared culture of ambition and achievement.'

REFLECTIVE EXERCISE: Find your employees' purpose

Ask each of your employees what matters to them, then find a way to enable them to achieve their purpose within the broader purpose of your organisation.

Your leadership style matters

Put any team in a burning house and tell them they can only escape by working together. What do you think will happen?[14] All the normal politics will go out of the window. Not to mention any shyness about saying what needs to be said for fear of upsetting others. No one will be manoeuvring to make themselves look good or flattering the CEO to protect their ego. 'No boss, I'm sure you'll work it out, given enough time.' Everything pales into insignificance when fighting for your life.

The reality is, our people are under pressure all the time. They are expected to do more with less. Budgets are tight, projects are ambitious and hours long. This is especially so in any disruptive (or survival) scenario, where you can also add in the imperative to succeed quickly before the status quo crushes the idea, or another disruptor slips in ahead of you. When there is a big job to be done, it is instinctive for a leader to push everyone harder. This might get things moving in the short term, but in the long run it will be counterproductive.

Yes, some people are resilient and applying pressure can act as a catalyst. They'll be inspired to do their best work, much in the same way as a boxer who, when cornered, is able to fight their way out. They draw on unseen depths of resources and thrive in the face of challenge. For others, though, such pressure is harmful. When confronted with pressure to work longer hours, quickly adapt to changing priorities and deliver on impossible deadlines, all against a backdrop of a crippling lack of resources to get the job done, increased anxiety and stress follow. Left unchecked, there is a long-tail result that negatively impacts mental and physical health. This manifests in things like broken relationships, addictions, obesity, long-term health conditions, insomnia, debt, bullying behaviours and many more negative outcomes. There is not a sane leader in the world who would choose this for their employees.

When it comes to disruptive leadership, you don't need to be a hero. We need to move on from the days when leadership was synonymous with the hero narrative. The cliché of the army commander 'born' to be a leader, fearlessly leading his troops into battle, standing tall under bombardment, unafraid and mysteriously escaping harm is no longer relevant. (These depictions were typically always men.) Nor are the Marvel superheroes, from Iron Man to Captain America to Thor, although the popularity of this franchise shows how pervasive this hero thinking still is. There are many examples in corporate history that show how this egotistical, controlling style of leadership is ultimately destructive. These are the leaders who come to the fore, create a flash fire, enjoy the fanfare and adulation and then disappear in a puff of smoke.

Think, for example, of Dick Fuld, once known as the 'Gorilla of Wall Street', who aggressively steered the historic Lehman Brothers investment bank into the murky world of subprime mortgages, ensuring its eventual and spectacular collapse at the height of the 2008 financial crisis.[15] Fuld followed in the footsteps of Ken Lay and Jeff Skilling who ruthlessly grew Enron from a small-time gas company to a $7 billion dollar darling of Wall Street, before filing for bankruptcy in 2001. Along the way, Skilling instigated the infamous 'rank and yank' culture, where the 'bottom' 15% of staff would lose their jobs each year. The only way of guaranteeing you kept your job was to make money, with bonuses or advancement not dependent on ethical or social behaviours.[16] In the UK, Sir Philip Green, once the darling of the fashion world, whose brands included Topshop, Burton and Miss Selfridge, saw his reputation irredeemably tarnished when his empire collapsed in November 2020 amid allegations of abuse and bullying of staff. Thousands lost their jobs and former workers of his BHS and Arcadia brands faced an uncertain future, with their pensions hanging in the balance.

The above are some examples of charismatic leaders whose actions often reflect the narcissistic leadership style, which can be defined as leaders who have 'grandiose belief systems and leadership styles, and are generally motivated by their needs for power and admiration rather than empathetic concern for the constituents and institutions they lead'.[17] There are many other, earlier examples: Andrew Carnegie, John D. Rockefeller, Henry Ford and Jack Welch[18] – all disruptors of their time. No doubt you will know of more recent examples. As we have seen, such ruthless leadership tactics are risky and frequently end spectacularly badly. Narcissists are typically emotionally isolated and highly distrustful, despite their effectiveness. A lack of self-awareness and restraining anchors results in high-risk strategies. They nurture grand schemes, become unrealistic dreamers and wrongly believe that only circumstances or enemies are blocking their success. It is this tendency towards grandiosity and distrust that is the Achilles' heel of narcissism, the idea that, 'Only I can do this.' This is not so. To be successful in the short and long term, as measured by doing good, a disruptive leader needs to carry their team with them.

Leadership trait research has shown that negative behavioural dispositions such as narcissism can be constrained by highly constraining 'strong' situations (strong behavioural norms, strong incentives for specific types of behaviours, and clear expectations concerning what behaviours will be rewarded and punished).[19]

In my work with leaders demonstrating narcissistic behaviours (and let's be honest, most of us have narcissistic tendencies), I tend to focus on two key areas: accountability and personal development.

Most of us don't really like being accountable. We'd much rather we had the freedom to do as we please and ask that you trust us. For someone with narcissistic tendencies, anyone who holds them to account is perceived much as a petulant child would a parent laying down the law. Get out of my way. You are stopping me. You don't understand. Narcissists manipulate, cajole, and influence to get their way. And they are very good at it.

Ensuring a power structure that effectively stops bad decisions and bad behaviours is critical for all of us, even more so to constrain narcissistic tendencies. For those of us who just want to get on and do, ensuring we have a safety mechanism to apply brakes to our decisions (which can harm self and others) is essential.

Do you hire and promote people who say yes to you? Is your leadership team scared of challenging you? When was the last time someone said something challenging to you? How did you respond? Do you listen to others, or do you always know best? Accepting a strong sense of accountability helps ground our feelings of grandeur.[20]

Personal development is the other key area to work on – a deep dive into ourselves. What makes us, us? Why do we behave the way we do? How do others perceive us? Where's the gap? Where are the growth areas?

Often narcissists have great charisma. Much has been written on this subject elsewhere, but as with any great strength, there is a corresponding weakness. With great light comes deep shadows. Don't be the leader who doesn't care. Who thinks the ends justify the means. When measured over time, our ability to make decisions and act in ways congruent with deeper purpose and the good of humanity is key to enduring greatness. I will deal with this subject more in Part Two.

REFLECTIVE EXERCISE: Leadership awareness

Thinking in terms of your work context, rate yourself on how much you agree with the following statements (0 is not at all, 10 is completely).

- I need to have all the answers
- I need to be perfect
- I can't show weakness
- I often know best
- I'm special, better than others
- I take challenge as a personal attack
- People feel safe challenging my ideas
- I value accountability

What do your answers say about you? Which questions relate to a hero style, and which ones to a narcissistic one? Are you happy with your answers? Would your best friend, or closest colleague agree with your answers?

Who can you explore your leadership style with, without judgement?

You may not consider yourself in the hero mould or recognise narcissistic tendencies. Yet our world is more complex than ever. The pace of technology alone doubles every year. AI threatens our existence, offshoring is common practice, the gig economy has taken hold and, following the pandemic, more people are working from home. Russia's invasion of Ukraine turned the globalist ideal on its head. The role and definition of 'leader' is far more fluid than previously. It has to be. Top-down command and control hierarchies are being replaced with a more collaborative and purpose-driven leadership style.

Do you know when to lead and when to follow? Do you recognise when to speak and when it's best to shut up and listen? Are you happy to sometimes allow your team to follow their own ideas and push back against yours? Are you prepared to accept that purpose is of greater importance than ego? These are all crucial factors in recognising the inherent worth, skills and expertise of others and knowing when they are more suited to the task at hand, so you can give them your full support. Admitting you don't have all the answers immediately makes you more approachable. When you invest in others like this, it doesn't just fuel your purpose, it also reduces the risk of failure.

When we get it right as leaders, our places of work become more pleasant. Employees will be engaged when they are recognised as the resourceful, intelligent and insightful people they are. Though the responsibility will always be yours, seeking the perspective of others and engaging them in your decisions benefits everyone. The ability to both attract and bring out the best in people is an important leadership skill and key to long-term positive disruption.

I've focused on the hero or narcissistic leader thus far. Even if these don't relate to you, I'd like to invite you to reflect on your own leadership style.

REFLECTIVE EXERCISE: Your leadership style

Write down ten descriptive words to describe your leadership style. Then ask your team to do the same (anonymously).

Now consider:

- Where are the gaps?
- What can/will you do about that difference?
- What strategies can you put in place to mitigate your weaknesses, while accentuating your strengths? (This might include finding mentors, working with a coach, verbalising your development goals to a manager or sharing more authentically with your team.)

Cash is king

The second type of fuel necessary for any organisation's success is cash. Cash really does make the world go round. The global market capitalisation (total value of publicly listed companies) is circa $100 trillion, with the USA contributing approximately 40%

of that number. In America, two-thirds of employees work for private (non-listed) companies, giving an idea of the size of the private market. It is estimated that over 50% of the investment in plant and equipment is made by these same private companies.[21] As startups grow, they require further investment rounds to fuel their ambition. Cash allows them to invest in people, research and development, marketing and infrastructure in order to grow. In times of recession, cash dries up, cutting off the life flow.

Despite its prevalence, there are many misunderstandings about money. This is something of which I have had first-hand experience. In 2002, following a decade of consulting with the likes of Lloyd's of London, Axa Insurance and British Telecom, I started my own IT consultancy firm. We grew quickly, resulting in a global client base and two office locations (including London) managing and supporting large IT programmes worth hundreds of millions of pounds within financial services firms such as Halifax Bank of Scotland (HBOS), Barclays, JP Morgan and UBS. We also worked with central and local government and manufacturing firms. We were in the same league as IBM and PwC. What we lacked in size, we made up for in passion.

When we were still tiny and living hand to mouth, one client paid us £125,000 in advance for twelve months of service, simply because I had the brass neck to ask for it. Without that substantial cash injection, and others like it, we would never have been able to grow as quickly as we did. Unfortunately, as we discovered, rapid growth is not always a cause for celebration. When my business took off like a rocket, it wasn't finding customers that was the problem, it was cash flow. A company can be profitable yet fail for lack of liquidity. Burn through cash without a return and you go bust. Corporate graveyards are littered with cash-poor companies.

I had fallen into the same trap that I have seen many business owners stuck in. I believed revenue constituted success. As the well-known saying goes, revenue is vanity, profit sanity, but cash is king. It's always cash. Cash in your bank. Cash means options. No cash – no options, no company.

If you've had cash flow problems you will be familiar with the dread of not knowing whether you can make the next payroll, or tax bill. There is a reason companies have 60, 90 or even 120-day payment terms. They use their creditors (suppliers) to bankroll their company. It's free money. This is exactly what we had to do. We learned to reduce our own payment terms, pay creditors later where appropriate and, when things were really tight, we delayed paying tax bills as the penalty was nothing compared to the liquidity it provided. When I took a sabbatical, I received daily emails giving me the cash position and forecast. No cash, no company.

Once we got back on track, my accountant advised me to ask banks for money even when we didn't need it. She was right. Where possible, all businesses should seek out loans and investments way before they get into difficulty. Have a daily cash flow forecast, with projected cash flows over the next year by month. Some businesses will need this by the week, day or even hour. Disciplined monitoring could save the life of any company.

No business is immune to the tyranny of cash flow. It's also not a rule that the bigger you get, the easier it gets. Look at the example of Tesla, under the leadership of one of the world's best-known disruptors, Elon Musk. This is someone who passionately believes the world needs electric cars, but he also understands that to disrupt on a large scale requires large amounts of money. Musk has often spoken honestly about the stress he finds himself under. In 2017 he tweeted, 'The reality is great highs, terrible lows and unrelenting stress. Don't think people want to hear about the last two.'[22] Notably, 2017 was the year Tesla briefly overtook both Ford Motor Company and General Motors in market capitalisation, and in June appeared in the Fortune 500 list for the first time. Behind this success story was a business burning through cash at an alarming rate. In the same year, Bloomberg reported that, 'Over the past 12 months, the electric-car maker has been burning money at a clip of about $8,000 a minute (or $480,000 an hour)' preparing for Model 3.[23] That's the equivalent of $1bn a quarter. It is hardly surprising, then, that in an interview with the *New York Times*, Musk said, 'This past year has been the most difficult and painful year of my career. It was excruciating.'[24]

As these various interviews and profiles show, the list of sacrifices Musk has made for his business is long: he regularly works 120-hour weeks, spending days at the Tesla factory without going outside. He doesn't have enough time to see much of his children or friends and has spent birthdays in the office.

Arianna Huffington, founder and CEO of the *Huffington Post*, who has spoken openly about her own burnout, wrote Musk an open letter pleading with him to gain balance.[25] Elon Musk's response, sent at 2.32am, said simply: 'Ford & Tesla are the only two American car companies to avoid bankruptcy. I just got home from the factory. You think this is an option. It is not.'[26]

Elon perfectly demonstrates the amount of energy required to drive global disruption. (I personally always felt his purchase and stint as CEO of Twitter (or X) was a distraction, regardless of the marketing power it bought him.)

But what, then, is the key to managing money efficiently and raising cash where required, while keeping a sense of balance? Once again, having a strong sense of purpose is key. Maran Nelson, co-founder and CEO of Clara Labs, has raised $7.2m for her artificial intelligence assistant business to date. The secret to raising finance, Nelson says, is:

'…really fundamentally believing in what you are doing, like knowing it is good. You have to know that it needs to exist in the world, and in you knowing that you set yourself apart. Very few people know that what they are doing is great.'[27]

When financial pressures escalate, it is crucial to create a clear road map to find a way through the challenges. This was the strong message I got from Kate Ringrose, CFO of the UK energy giant Centrica (and owner of British Gas), a business that at the time of writing is facing threats on a number of fronts. First, there has been a global rise in gas prices, which has hit its UK customer base especially hard thanks to the country's reliance on fossil fuels. Higher gas prices have led to over a third of the UK's energy suppliers going out of business in a short space of time, leading to Centrica taking on around 700,000 customers from failed suppliers and picking up the cost of onboarding them. Meanwhile, the business is under pressure to invest substantially in sustainable solutions to meet future energy needs. The way to navigate through this, according to Kate Ringrose, is with dexterity and a sense of balance, as well as a solid plan.

'This is an industry that matters at every single level. On any given day, I can be as concerned about someone who is struggling with heating bills as with the geopolitics of a region I am never likely to visit, as well as the future of the planet. Ultimately, there are lots of different lenses that we are viewed through, by many different people, whether it is engineers, investors or customers, and each one has a different dynamic. What I do is try and bring those elements together. My role as the CFO is to tell the story of the company through numbers.

'An analogy that I use with my team is to visualise where we are as a group on a map. We can see where we are on this map, and where we believe we could go, given the various different choices and how they could play out. This helps orientate the group to our position today. When we talk about market contexts, dynamics or strategic choices, the map makes it easier to see where each one could take us. We can look at different events and isolate the things that could help us or hinder us most. It helps in articulating the impact that those events might, or might not, have, depending on what we want to do and where we want to be. It helps orientate and anchor us and allows us to be more dexterous in our response.

'This approach enables us to make choices in terms of what capital we have, and how we want to spend that cash to make sure that we've got a good balance of risk that can allow us to prosper in all sorts of different commodity environments. That is really important. Right now, customers care about affordability. However, something that is also a priority is the responsibility that we have towards our planet in terms of the environment. We have to balance short-term and long-term priorities when making choices to ensure we are a sustainable company for the future.'

While cash is king and essential to fuel growth and disruption, it comes at a cost. As Kate shows, things are never easy when it comes to money and tough choices need to be made. But these choices need to be made fairly, strategically and in the interest of all stakeholders. Stability and, ultimately, the ability to disrupt, comes out of having a strong cash position. This is the foundation that will allow you to look at the market in a different way.

REFLECTIVE EXERCISE: Cash

Think about the statement, 'Revenue is vanity, profit sanity, but cash is always king'. Consider:

- What does cash mean to you personally?
- What is the cash position of your own venture?
- What actions can you take to improve cash flow?
- What importance does cash have in your strategy?
- How can you get more of it?
- Where are you using a lack of cash as an excuse not to achieve more?
- What might be an alternative way to achieve more, regardless of cash?

Cash doesn't guarantee success or employee engagement

Money is nearly always seen as the answer. Start-ups want it, investors provide it and new products swallow it. Throw enough cash at an issue with your disruptive plan and it will succeed. People not buying it? Spend more. Product not good enough? Spend more. Whatever the resistance – spend more. But cash alone does not generate success. You cannot force a new offering onto an unresponsive market. Cash is simply one component of many that lead to success. You need leadership (heat), fuel (the team and money) and oxygen (customers). It is how you, the leader, marshal these resources over time that matters most. The fire you create cannot be listed on a profit and loss statement, nor a balance sheet. Yet without it, the organisation is dead, regardless of the numbers. Much as we might want more cash, it does not protect us from poor decision-making, lack of a clear focus or the absence of discipline.

The story of Carillion is a case in point. Carillion was once the UK's second-largest construction company. It had 43,000 global employees (20,000 in the UK) and held many government contracts for building and managing schools and hospitals. It had also been awarded the coveted high-speed rail contract, HS2. In 2016, it recorded revenues of £5.2bn ($6.8bn) and a market capitalisation of £1bn ($1.3bn). All to no avail. Borrowings had increased to £1.5bn ($2bn) when the banks pulled the plug in January 2018 and Carillion collapsed.[28]

Following the inevitable government enquiry, the committee chair, Rachel Reeves, MP for Leeds West, described the leadership of Carillion as 'delusional directors' saying their 'colossal failure as managers' had 'effectively pressed the self-destruct button on the company.'[29] There was no pulling of punches here. Cash wasn't the issue – leadership was.

Corporate history is littered with failed businesses that attempted to throw money at problems, rather than sort out the actual issue: poor leadership. In 1988, RJR Nabisco invested the equivalent of $700m in today's money into something entirely new: smoke-less cigarettes. After launching to much fanfare, the product was withdrawn after four months. 'It tastes like shit and smells like a fart,' said RJR Nabisco's boss F Ross Johnson, adding, 'We spent $350 million and we ended up with a turd with a tip.'[30]

In 1996, McDonald's introduced a gourmet burger they called the Arch Deluxe. It was launched to appeal to 'urban sophisticates' outside of their target demographic. McDonald's spent $100 million on advertising, more than it had ever spent on a campaign before.[31] It flopped. Today, there are gourmet burger places on almost every city street. The time for 'urban sophisticates' has finally arrived.

Even the top CEOs in the world sometimes make mistakes. By 2014, Amazon had invested four years of research and development into its new Amazon Fire Phone. It was Jeff Bezos' baby. He had spent a month of his own time working as the product manager on the project and had signed off on 'surreal amounts of money' to add new features.[32] It bombed and is widely seen as Bezos' biggest flop. Just thirteen months after the launch, Amazon retired from phone manufacturing, writing off $170 million (£131m) of inventory. The total R&D costs are unknown.

If cash does not guarantee success, can it guarantee employee engagement? The answer is a firm no. No employee gets out of bed to generate a return for shareholders. Your employees don't bounce through the front door to your business each day desperate to make you wealthier. Even compensation schemes that pay out based on achieving financial targets will only take you so far with engaging employees.

Cash is not king when it comes to engagement. We see evidence of this all the time. When a key employee hands in their notice and is offered a significant financial inducement to stay, they won't do so if they were disengaged to look elsewhere enough in the first place. The key to engagement, as explained earlier in the chapter, is to articulate your purpose clearly, align this with an employee's own purpose and practise good management.

The moment money becomes the focus, purpose takes a back seat. So do ethics. In its rawest form, being driven by money alone results in the worst of human and corporate behaviours. Values fly out of the window and shady deals, corruption, pension fund drains, kickbacks and exploitation of the powerless become the norm.

For a disruptive leader, the two biggest sources of fuel to start a fire are people and cash. But it is not a given that either will produce the desired effect simply by existing. Careful thought needs to be given to how you release their potential. If you get it right, your team will drive incredible results. In the right environment, they are a renewable energy source. Engaging them in a meaningful purpose is about the most fulfilling process possible. To engage, we not only need a crystal clear and compelling purpose, but it needs to be well communicated. Communication is far more than just words; it is how we live our lives, day in and day out. It's in our decisions, our focus and where we expend our energy.

To highlight the importance of employee engagement: companies with an engaged workforce are 21% more profitable,[33] companies in the USA lose $450–$550 billion each year due to disengaged workers alone, and companies with a thriving corporate culture can achieve over four times higher revenue growth.[34]

Cash is essential for all businesses, but it isn't the sole ingredient needed for success. Laser-focused attention on achieving purpose in line with values will enable you to most effectively prioritise your cash spend, informing your hires, programmes and people. Keep an eye on cash but don't let it become your sole focus – that is a slippery slope to the wrong sort of headlines and possibly the end of a business.

REFLECTIVE EXERCISE: Employee engagement

Look at the questions below and give an answer between 0% and 100%.

- How many of those you lead can state your purpose accurately?
- How aligned are they with your purpose and sense of urgency?
- What could you do differently to increase engagement levels?

(Hint: what's in it for them?)

4
Oxygen

M uch as we need oxygen to live, so does fire. No oxygen, no fire.[35] Oxygen is needed to start your fire and to keep it burning. In disruptive leadership, that oxygen is your market. Your community. It is the customers for your idea, product or service. Those you seek to impact. Oxygen is what will fan the flames and grow the fire. Cut off that supply and all that will remain is a smouldering ruin and dying embers. This is exactly what happened to Monster.com which, over a less than twenty-year period, went from hero to, well, not quite zero, but almost.

In 1999, Monster.com's rapid disruption of the recruitment sector was sealed by its first Super Bowl advert, entitled 'When I Grow Up'. In the ad, kids delivered powerful statements to job seekers by declaring, 'When I grow up, I want to be a yes man,' or, 'I want to claw my way into middle management.' Monster's message was clear: you deserve a better job. Everything else in your life will flow from there. Indeed, founder Jeff Taylor's mantra was: 'It's half about a better job and half about a better life.'[36]

The strong message found its mark among job hunters. By 2000, the Monster.com website was valued at more than $8 billion, with shares trading at $91 at their peak after entering the stock market at $7 a share just three years earlier. In 2006, it was one of the twenty most visited websites in the world. All this from a company that launched in 1994, initially copying newspaper job ads onto their website from a tiny unit above a Chinese restaurant in Boston.

Monster had a lot going for it when it came to disrupting the recruitment market. For a start, it had 'first mover' advantage, since it was the first public job search website on the internet. It also offered the first public CV/resume database in the world and was the first to feature job search agents or job alerts. Most of all, though, its founding purpose of helping people find jobs was a noble endeavour that resonated with its growing customer base.

Fast forward to 2011 and Monster was rated the worst stock of the year. In 2016, it was acquired by Amsterdam-based recruitment firm Randstad Holdings for $429 million, a fraction of its peak value. To illustrate the extent of its fall from grace, compare the valuation with that of rival LinkedIn, which was sold to Microsoft for $26 billion in the same year. LinkedIn was not even profitable, whereas Monster was. What had happened?

Quite simply, Monster had lost sight of its noble purpose, the difference it wanted to make. In 2007, Monster trod the well-worn path of an organisation seeking to protect what it had built (the new status quo). On appointment, the new CEO, Sal Iannuzzi, replaced purpose with financial targets. In subsequent Monster town halls he would reiterate his goal of increasing stock price. There was no mention of a better job and better life. Nothing about job seekers. No focus on helping customers, or improving the industry. Under pressure to drive the numbers, Iannuzzi eroded the thing that had attracted customers in the first place. The disruptor had lost sight of its purpose, and in the process had lost heat, fuel and completely starved the company of oxygen.

When I work with leaders of organisations, a question I often ask is, 'What is it you want?' The answer that invariably follows is a financial target.

'Why do you want to grow?' I press. This question is almost always met with a look that suggests I am a bit of an idiot. When they realise that I'm serious, the replies are usually along the lines of:

- 'To be the biggest.'
- 'To gain market share.'
- 'Isn't that what's expected?'

Each of these answers reveals a risk of falling into the same trap Monster did. Financial targets mean nothing to most employees. As I detailed in the previous chapter, no employee goes to work to make someone else rich (unless in the process they will become rich them-selves). Putting profit first also alienates customers.

Put yourself in the shoes of a customer for a moment. If you are loyal to a business, you become accustomed to their level of engagement and service. If that engagement drops off, or the firm begins to cut corners as it aggressively seeks to grow its bottom line, it grates. You may stick with that business for a little while, imagining it is maybe having an off day, or week. But if it goes on too long, you'll vote with your feet. Most likely, you'll move onto a business that does offer you what you have come to expect. If the new supplier is even better, that seals the fate of the old one. You'll never go back. The disruptor has been disrupted.

Playing it safe and managing risk

If focusing on increasing revenue growth is fraught with danger, so is playing it safe. I once worked with the owners of a mid-sized professional services firm. After presiding over three years of over 20% year-on-year growth, they decided it was time to take their metaphorical foot off the accelerator. 'We've decided to play safe this year,' they told me. 'Instead of focusing on growth, we will focus on cost cutting to maintain profits.' Despite my challenge, they were adamant about the change in strategy. Rapid growth had brought its own challenges, they told me. It was time to retrench and stabilise.

It didn't take long before the cracks in this strategy began to show. Customers noticed an absence of innovation. The cuts in marketing spend meant the firm was not getting its message across. Nimbler rivals were swooping in to take advantage of the slowdown and began to erode their market share. The team were noticeably less engaged, since they were nervous and unsettled about the abrupt change of direction, which had a knock-on effect on the customers they worked with. Within months, the figures made for gloomy reading. Not only had revenues eroded, so had profits. It didn't take much prodding from me for the owners to revert to the original dynamic, a high-growth strategy and, by acting quickly, they recovered.

Playing it safe is like turning off the boiler in your house in the autumn. As time ticks by, the pleasant heat that warmed the place during summer gives way to a pervasive dampness. With damp comes mould. Tiny spores travel through the house, entering every room, giving the lick of death to wood, joists and plaster. It will smell terrible, furniture and fixings will be ruined and your once beloved house will fall steadily into disrepair.

Safety whispers seductively. 'The status quo is easier. You've gone far enough. Stop pushing. Stop making waves. Stop taking risks. You've made it. Protect shareholder return. Enjoy what you have.' Give into these thoughts and you will starve your business of oxygen.

REFLECTIVE EXERCISE: Identify your priorities

What are you prioritising right now? Is protecting what you have more important than growth? If so – are you clear as to why?

None of this is to say that business should be conducted recklessly. Disruption should be planned carefully, with a firm eye on the balance between risk and reward. This is bread and butter to Wan Norashikin Mohd Nasir, the global vice president of risk management and business continuity management at Indorama Ventures, a chemical company and the world's largest producer of PET resins. While headquartered in Thailand, the organisation has 147 sites in 38 countries spread across the world and is, therefore, constantly subject to a range of threats, from war to political change, to natural disasters, any of which can suck the oxygen from the business almost overnight. Wan, known as Nonie, says there is no way to remove risks altogether, but that if you acknowledge their existence you can prepare and respond more effectively. She told me:

'If the organisation has the right governance foundation and the right processes in place, then it won't catch you off guard. If you have these mechanisms, and then consider what else might happen, it reduces the impact. Change is an opportunity, though. If you are

growing a business, you can't be risk averse
or fear risk. Leaders simply can't only manage
what they are comfortable with. The business
landscape is constantly changing and evolving.
If we embrace change, we can stay ahead of
the game, be world-class and maintain our
competitive advantage.'

It is critical to understand what can cut off the oxygen
to your fire. Nonie, who helped design Indorama's
risk leadership programme, says there are two types
of risk. The first is operational. These are the day-to-
day risks that might seem mundane, but are important
to manage. The second type of risk are those strategic
risks that, left unattended, can impact the long-term
viability of the business. In both cases, risk mitigation
works best if the problem is broken down into pieces
and each is dealt with in a timely fashion. This means
a swift and comprehensive assessment, followed by
quick decisions – or, as Nonie puts it, 'connecting
the dots' – informed by pulling the right information
together. It was this systematic approach that put her
former employer PETRONAS out ahead when Covid-
19 first appeared. Reflecting on that time, Nonie
told me:

'It was January 2020 when I first heard about
this virus in Wuhan, China. It would have
been easy to dismiss it at the time because
the nearest business was in Malaysia. The
first thing we did, though, was to look at the

potential worst-case scenario. By February, there were a number of cases in Italy where we had two plants. It didn't impact our business plans but I triggered the executive vice president, who is very strategic, to create the key business case and discuss the potential impact on the supply chain. What would be the worst that could happen if it did reach us? I call it a risk conversation, where we focus on all the probable scenarios that could impact us and ask ourselves what we should do about them.

'It was a couple of weeks after that conversation that the virus began to spread. By this stage we had set up our Covid-19 taskforce, with a strategy for all our petrochemical, lubricant plants, refinery, retail and trading outfits. By the time it hit us, we had our response fully developed. A lot of businesses emulated our approach.

'The risk strategy was tested again when Russia invaded Ukraine, and I'm pleased to say it stood up well.'

When an organisation has a 'risk mindset', with the relevant frameworks in place, it means the right decisions can be made quickly when a crisis appears. It also means leaders don't need to constantly 'hold back' for fear of putting themselves in a risky situation they can't get out of.

REFLECTIVE EXERCISE: Risk

Answer the following questions:

- Is risk on your agenda?
- What might steal your oxygen?
- What's your attitude to and appetite for risk?
- Do you have a structured approach to managing risk?

The prevailing conditions

Skilful leaders are able to read the market and respond appropriately. Wildfires are a perfect analogy here. The reason California experiences wildfires is down to a mix of unique climate and topographical conditions. It is a heavily forested region and, in summer and autumn, temperatures are exceptionally high. Add into the mix the Santa Ana, a katabatic wind, which moves from the high-pressure heat of the Great Basin and upper Mojave Desert, towards low pressure over the Pacific Ocean. As the wind is funnelled through mountain passes, its temperature increases by 10°C (50°F) for every 1,000m (3,300 feet) it descends. When in full force, the coast and plains are hotter than the deserts. As it warms, the wind's ability to hold moisture increases, which reduces its relative humidity.[37] Add together the fuel (dry forested areas) and oxygen (the hot wind), and there only needs to be a single stray spark from a barbeque, a downed powerline, or even a deliberate act of arson, and a catastrophe can rapidly unfold.

In chapter one, when we spoke about spontaneous combustion, we learned that disruptive success can often be down to being in the right place at the right time. Somehow, like the Californian wildfires, the conditions are just right for an explosive end result. This is perhaps too simplistic an explanation, so let's break it down further. In *Outliers*, Malcolm Gladwell demonstrates that for those who gain success, it tends to be the product of unique history (cultural, genetic, financial), luck (unique advantages/opportunities not available to others) and sheer hard work.[38]

For unique history, consider when and where a leader was born and the relative advantage or disadvantage that shaped their early years. Gladwell notes that the majority of top players in Canadian hockey teams have birthdays between January and March. Why is this significant? The Canadian school entry system is based on a cut-off date of 1 January. Just being a few months older when starting school, with the corresponding organised sports programmes, gives a significant advantage to kids born at the start of the year. This point about fortuitous timing also applies more broadly to the era we find ourselves in. Gladwell highlights that Bill Gates, the founder of Microsoft, was born at the right time (at the beginning of the digital age) and in the right place and thus, as a teenager, had unique access to code mainframes.

When it comes to luck, this is where (often unexpected) outside factors can amplify the prospects of a business. An example here might be Airbnb, a business founded by two designers, Brian Chesky and Joe Gebbia, in 2008. Chesky and Gebbia couldn't afford the rent on their San Francisco apartment and came up with the idea of renting out three airbeds on their living room floor and offering to cook breakfast for their guests. The idea coincided with a design conference in the West Coast city, when all the hotels in the area were fully booked. They set up a simple blog to advertise Airbnb (a diminution of 'airbed B&B') and got three renters for $80 each. Sensing they were onto something, they enlisted the help of a former flatmate, and computer science graduate, Nathan Blecharczyk.[39]

Without wishing to detract from the idea for the business, there was an element of lucky timing involved. Not only was the world just waking up to the 'sharing' economy, but Airbnb also launched in the midst of the worst financial crisis in a decade. For many startups, this might have been a worry, but for Airbnb, it was an advantage. People still wanted to travel but were less keen on paying the big bucks for smart hotels. This way, they could see the world and stay in cheaper accommodation that had the added bonus of being a little quirkier and more interesting than what they'd find in faceless chains. Meanwhile, numerous households saw an enticing new revenue stream from renting out their spare rooms, sofas, treehouses and even sheds. The external circumstances of an extreme financial downturn undoubtedly contributed to Airbnb's explosive growth.

Luck, of course, works both ways. The Covid-19 pandemic hit the business hard. In 2020, Airbnb saw a 39% drop in bookings as restrictions disrupted travel across the world. The business had initially planned its IPO for August that year but was forced to delay it after pandemic-related cancellations saw its value drop from a 2017 high of $31 billion, to around $18 billion. Available listings also dropped by 5%. In May 2020, the company laid off around 25% of its staff, leaving around 1,900 employees.[40]

REFLECTIVE EXERCISE: Luck

Think about the following questions, then answer them as honestly as possible:

- What luck do you currently have working in your favour?
- Where have you been lucky or unlucky?
- How well-equipped are you to take advantage of a lucky break, or adapt to any bad luck that comes your way?

The strongest prevailing wind that any business needs to be aware of is driven by customers and the markets. Public opinion is fickle, but it can make or break a business. This was something Australian businessman Mark Cutifani had to be acutely aware of when, in 2013, he joined the loss-making, debt-laden Anglo American plc as chief executive. Anglo American is one of the world's largest mining groups and, at that time, was the major producer of copper, iron ore and platinum. It was also battling with a brutal downturn in the commodity markets within a context of growing awareness around sustainability and environmental concerns.

Mark recognised the scale of the task in front of him – or, as he aptly put it, the 'burning platform' that needed urgent attention. Drawing on his own sense of purpose – to make a difference to the wider world and deliver a tangible outcome for Anglo American – Mark began an ambitious change programme. This programme began even before he joined the company, when he wrote an outside analysis of Anglo American, a document entitled 'Starting on the right foot'. He gave it to the board on day one, with the caveat that he didn't know how accurate it was, since he was working off reports of how the outside world saw the business. However, his analysis had raised a number of questions.

'My first impression of the organisation was that it had no sense of itself and what it could achieve with the resources that it had. By this I mean what it had in the ground, as well as people and skills. It was quite dysfunctional. I could see a whole range of things that would look like outcomes. The question became: how do you make changes to help people drive towards what that potential might be?'

In the first six months, Mark conducted an urgent asset review, realising that, in his words, 'If we don't shake our leg and get cracking, we're not going to be here for much longer.' It was clear there needed to be some tough calls. During this period, he changed half of the top leadership team and reduced the 160,000-strong workforce to 90,000. (I asked him how easy he had found this process – as he had spoken so matter of factly. As he answered, it was clear it had taken a huge emotional toll, something we often think leaders are immune to.) Even with the changes he'd wrought, the pressure was relentless. Commodity prices continued to drop and the programme they'd implemented to reduce the number of mining assets was not going to be enough. Meanwhile, the expectations of all stake-holders were high. Mark explained:

> 'If you look at the world today, the knowledge
> of what's happening is greater than it's ever
> been. That means people's expectations are so
> much higher and more progressive. If leaders
> don't deliver on expectations, then it's going
> to be far more difficult. We have to give an
> exceptional amount of time and attention
> to where the world is going and where the
> expectations are.'

No opportunities can be missed. Mark recalled an early meeting discussing the platinum mining division. Almost 80% of the meeting time was spent talking about a mine in South Africa, which was then losing

$50 an ounce. They were brainstorming how to turn the loss into a minimum $50 an ounce margin. Right at the end of the meeting, the issue of another mine was raised. This location was being mined at less than 40% of its capacity, with a $1000 an ounce margin.

'I couldn't believe we had spent 80% of our time talking about an asset that was losing fifty bucks an ounce, when we had this other one with a $1000 margin that could almost carry the whole business. If you want to make big changes, you need to shift the conversation.'

The hardest job of the turnaround was changing people's perceptions of what a mining company should look like, he told me.

'I had to lead people by shining a light on the pathway. My goal was to help everyone understand how they could be a part of the change. This business will continue to evolve and the complexity, knowledge and expectations will grow. That's both the biggest opportunity and the biggest challenge for leaders today. If you aren't at the forefront of change, you will disappoint your constituents.'

Anglo American is a very different company today. While it has reduced the number of mines – from sixty-eight when Mark Cutifani joined to thirty-seven in 2022 when he retired – its output is 10% higher.

It is not just the Anglo American shareholders that are seeing a brighter future. Those who are concerned about sustainability will see a business moving in the right direction. The Responsible Mining Index scores Anglo American with the highest marks in five out of six categories, including economic development, community wellbeing and environmental responsibility.[41] No wonder Mark is often referred to as the 'Patron Saint of Mining'. Dealing with the prevailing wind is challenging, but for those leaders who are prepared to disrupt and make the big changes, it is possible.

REFLECTIVE EXERCISE: Prevailing winds

Ask yourself:

- What is your equivalent of the 'fifty bucks an ounce' conversation?
- Are you and your team talking about the right things?
- Which way is the wind blowing in your industry?

Disruption takes time

Not every disruption will be an overnight success, even with the benefit of positive prevailing conditions. You will need to provide increasing amounts of oxygen as you try different strategies before your fire catches. Startups typically pivot, often more than once, from the initial strategy they apply in their pursuit of the all-important oxygen of customers.

Facebook was originally designed to allow Harvard students to compare two students' pictures side by side and decide who was more attractive.[42] Its original name was FaceMash, which then became TheFacebook, before it became a global success as Facebook (and with its more recent new strategy came another new name, Meta).

In disruption, there are always winners and losers. As a rule of thumb, the more disruptive the technology, the more it will be seen as a threat and actively resisted by the status quo, which will do everything it can to suck the oxygen out of the idea. It is protectionism. The status quo is a powerful cartel deeply motivated to keep control. The status quo is the disruptive leader's main enemy and makes achieving meaningful disruption tough.

Take self-driving cars. Tesla, led by Elon Musk, has expended significant energy over time (generating heat), attracted the world's top engineers and programmers along with billions in cash (their fuel) and has a market of early adopters (the buyers). But we have yet to see what true disruption looks like in this context. There is still major resistance on its way. How will employers, and the unions that represent them, respond when humans are no longer needed to drive trains, buses, lorries and taxis? How quickly will the required network of charging stations be rolled out globally? What government regulations will need to be overcome in each country? How will Tesla deal with a major collision resulting in multiple fatalities? And how will Tesla fare once other major car manufacturers enter the market in a serious way?

The status quo is real. It is exasperating and sucks your time and energy. Worse still, it stands in the way of progress. Imagine you develop an innovative medical treatment that will save tens of thousands of lives, but in the process it disrupts the revenue streams of major pharma companies. Do you think they would stand idly by? Or would they do everything in their power to stop your product coming to market (while they try and copy it)?

The status quo allows millions of pounds and dollars to be wasted on meaningless or wasteful projects. It disregards shocking customer service as long as the traditional way (and power) is preserved. It leads to outmoded thinking and delays progress in every sphere of life.

Thankfully, disruptors do break through. There are plenty of examples of disruptors changing nations, transforming the way we shop, travel, learn, entertain and, yes, even drive. To truly disrupt takes an inordinate amount of energy. There is, however, one way to make things a little easier for yourself: generate oxygen to fan the flames. In other words, recruit customers and create demand.

Generating oxygen

A common error amongst many startups or product launches is to seek to build perfection before trying to sell it. I've been guilty of this myself. Yet speak to any investor or venture capital firm, and their recommendation to (almost) any startup is, ship an imperfect product/service and build in line with what the customer wants.[43] The more people you get on side who are interested in and encouraged by your innovation, the larger the supply of oxygen you will have to help you push back against the status quo. Elon Musk is a master at this art, creating an almost cult status around Tesla (originally built using the Lotus Elise chassis), Hyperloop and SpaceX. Another disruptive leader who has always understood the power of marketing and word of mouth is Sir Richard Branson.

As chairman of the Virgin Group, Branson controls some 400 companies. His personal worth is estimated at $3 billion.[44] That's not bad for a self-made man whose first businesses were a student magazine and mail order record company. Branson realised early on that it would be impossible to put his Virgin brand on the world map through advertising alone. It was far too expensive. Instead, he became well-known for his publicity stunts. These stunts have included attempting to fly round the world, twice, in a hot air balloon and wearing a wedding dress to publicise Virgin Brides. He also drove a tank down New York's Fifth Avenue before firing a cannon at a Coca-Cola sign to publicise the launch of Virgin Cola. To celebrate Virgin Atlantic's first flight, he bungee-jumped off the 407-feet high Palms Hotel Casino in Las Vegas. He is a master of courting publicity to build a brand. Why is this important? A strong brand helps to create favourable conditions for your product or service – in other words, it provides much-needed oxygen.

Branson has explained his tactics, saying that publicity and getting your brand or company's name out and about is absolutely critical: 'I think that often a good PR story is far more effective than a full-page ad, and it's a hell of a lot cheaper.'

The bigger the idea, the more time and energy you will need to put into it. Branson spends 25% of his time on marketing, figuring out how to raise the Virgin brand. He also recommends that, if you get the chance to get in front of a TV camera, you should do it.[45] This is not the place for half-hearted attempts.

In the coming years, we are likely to see some extraordinary disruptive products, from wearable artificial intelligence to brain plugins that significantly improve memory and decision-making. There will be many more besides. Do you have what it takes to take big risks and possibly play the long game? To figure out how to gain increasing amounts of oxygen for your fire – even to create the prevailing conditions for your success?

REFLECTIVE EXERCISE: Where is your oxygen coming from?

Ask yourself the following questions:

- What's more important to you, perfection or purpose?

- How much time do you devote to speaking to, and listening to, your target market? Is it enough?

- How could you increase your oxygen by 10%?

- If the resistance is too great, how can you make headway within a niche?
- Is your marketing purpose-driven?
- What free publicity could you gain to raise your brand?

Now consider, what is your key takeaway from this chapter? What actions will you take as a result? Write them down.

PART TWO
MAINTAINING YOUR FIRE

5

Create The Conditions For Continuous Growth

'I spend all day every day in meetings, dealing with staff and the problems they cause,' opined an owner of a professional services firm. 'I'm working long hours but have no time for the things I know are important.'

In my next call I hear from a VP of product: 'I can't find the right staff and it's hurting my ability to do what we need. I'm working twelve-hour days, six days a week, but it is not enough.'

The call after that is with a general manager leading a region for a Fortune 100 company. 'My husband complains because I'm catching up on my emails when I go to bed. But it's the only time I have, and if I don't catch up then, when will I?'

Once we have a fire – either because we started it, or we join one – the challenge changes. Where previously all the energy (heat) was focused on gaining traction in your market, now there are staff and money (fuel) that need constant attention and demanding customers (oxygen) to keep happy. How do you balance your time? Where do you focus? What takes priority? And how do you ensure you don't burn out?

Extracting the gold

Imagine you are on holiday, cooling off your feet in a river. The warm sun glints across the surface of the gently flowing waterway and you smile as you look down and wriggle your toes. You notice a gleam in one of the rocks below and bend down to pick it up. Could it be? It certainly looks like it. It's gold!

Barely able to contain your excitement, you return to the edge of the river, retrieve your phone from beside your shoes and begin to search the internet. How do you tell if it is real gold? And if so, how much *actual* gold is there in that rock? Most importantly, how do you process it into something of value?

As you do your research, you discover that it is possible to retrieve and refine the gold yourself with just some basic tools. It's a process that has been practised for at least 10,000 years. Hardly able to contain your excitement, you order an acetylene blow torch, a graphite crucible to melt the gold in, tongs, a ladle and a mould. They'll be waiting for you when you get home.

Some days later, balancing your incandescent glee with a modicum of impatience, you place your impure gold into the crucible and fire up the blow torch. On applying heat directly to the lump, it begins to melt. Once it reaches a temperature above 1,064°C (1,947°F) you see what looks like glowing molten lava. You carefully pour the gold into the mould. Just as your research said they would, base metal impurities (copper, silver, iron, tin, lead, mercury and antimony) rise to the top. You scrape these off while still molten and leave what remains to cool. To your delight, you are left with a thick, coin-shaped lump of gold.

As a leader, your ability to refine 'gold' will be critical to the success of the next stage of your fire. Your focus will be on taking what is imperfect (whether it be strategy or systems, products or people, cash flow or your own skillset) and utilise an effective process of refinement to ensure a high-quality end product, without being too demanding in your pursuit of perfection.

How hot you burn as a leader is key to this refinement process. Ensuring the optimal levels of heat, fuel and oxygen requires an awareness of how hot you yourself blow. Lukewarm leaders create lukewarm environments. These are not the organisations that outperform their competitors. The pace is slow, standards low and expectations mediocre. The impurities remain (and increase over time). The opposite is also true. Apply too much heat by ratcheting up the pressure too high and the fire will be too hot. People around you will burn out. There is a reason startups fail in such high numbers and demanding leaders have a reputation for being terrible at people management.

The pressure to work long hours, without respite, typically results in disengagement and broken lives.

To extract gold from rock, as we did with our imaginary holiday find, the rock first has to be crushed to separate out the gold. As leaders, we have to figure out the right amount of pressure that will bring out the best of our people without decimating them. Similarly, when we place our gold in a furnace to purify it, we don't want to blow too hot, as even metal will burn at a high enough temperature. There is a fine line between developing talent to achieve the extraordinary, and burning them out.

Quality leadership at every level is key to an organisation finding the right balance between allowing dross to remain and causing burnout. Just one component required is emotional intelligence (often referred to as EQ). EQ has been regularly cited as the difference between great and poor leadership and has many definitions. My working definition of EQ is: an awareness of self, mastery of one's own emotions, awareness of others and awareness of one's impact on others. The awareness of your impact on others is a critical component of empathy. Empathy can be defined as the ability to understand and share the feelings of another. It's the equivalent of walking in another's shoes to understand their experience better.

This got me thinking about the interviews with leading international CEOs, conducted by my business partner Katie Litchfield, for the *WeQual Unfiltered CEO* podcasts. Katie asks each leader a seemingly benign question: what makes a good leader? In some ways, it's an unfair question because the subject is so vast, with no perfect, black-and-white answer. Yet, of all the answers these leaders could have given, most interviewees immediately identified two keys to success. First, surrounding yourself with highly talented people and releasing them to achieve a purpose; and second, a need for empathy.

Even though I have coached on this subject for fifteen years, the fact that empathy was mentioned so often surprised me. Central to growing a fire is good leadership, and the leader's level of EQ is hugely important here. I'm curious to know: would EQ be on your list of what makes a good leader?

Less than one-third of employees are engaged at work – which means most managers who read this have some disengaged employees. The solution lies in developing increased EQ; below is a practical, quick exercise to help you do this.

REFLECTIVE EXERCISE: One of the team

Imagine you wake up tomorrow as a member of your team (if you don't have staff, imagine you are a supplier or customer). Who is this person? Give them a name and a face. Spend 30 seconds thinking about this person and place yourself in their shoes.

- How do you feel when you wake up?
- As you think about your day ahead, is there a sense of excitement, apathy or dread?
- As you go about your day, what causes you frustration? Do you have the resources you need to

do your job? Do you feel empowered, able to make decisions and make progress? Or are you stifled, micromanaged, not trusted? Can you challenge your manager's viewpoint?

- What hours are you working? Are you exhausted? Are you clear on your role? When was the last time you received encouragement or support? Do you feel energised or exhausted? Driven or defeated?

Spend a minute or two thinking through your answers.

What will you do differently with your new empathetic perspective?

Removing organisational and personal dross

From an organisational perspective, reviewing the competition, trends in the market, and current performance can result in a need to make tough decisions to repurpose, restructure, sell or shut down service lines or even entire divisions. If we don't constantly prioritise the process of refining our gold we allow the build-up of impurities (organisational and personal dross) that drag our results down.

Disruptive leaders keep the pressure on, and pressure, as we've seen, increases heat. The more heat, the hotter the fire. The hotter the fire, the more impurity is removed. Anything that slows progress is reviewed, refined, cut off or improved, with the sole intention of keeping the fire burning hot. The mantra is simple: increase the heat, fuel and oxygen.

But how do we ensure we burn with the right amount of heat? Organisational effectiveness is a direct result of leadership effectiveness. If there is no step change in leadership effectiveness, it is us that becomes the blocker. The process of refinement applies as much to us as others. First, we must learn to let go. The path to leadership maturity is a long one. The first casualty has to be our ego. Remaining technically or functionally brilliant is likely to be one of your biggest barriers to envisioning and empowering *others* to achieve. One C-suite member in a FTSE 50 company recently told me, 'I work too hard, I can't stop. I haven't seen a friend in three years, I have no hobbies, I just work. That's all I do.' She has yet to make the leap from 'me' to 'we'. For many powerful but historical reasons she believes her success is predicated on doing what has made her successful in the past. But leadership is about leading others to achieve greatness, not about personal brilliance.

Chances are you excelled (or still do) in a specific area. You got really, really good at something – whether in sales, marketing, legal, finance, technology, risk, HR, etc. It's the reason you were promoted, or it's the reason you started your own business. But as your responsibilities increase (and your fire grows), your strength becomes your Achilles' heel. It's one of the hardest steps you make – letting go of the thing that made you successful.

In my first business, I wanted to promote a fantastic technical consultant to become my operations director. His immediate fear? 'If I move away from being technical, I will lose my skillset and you will be able to fire me more easily.' This is a common fear, and is worthy of consideration.

This person did not see the value in being a great manager. Yet as we move into management, even more so into leadership positions, those of us who try to keep a hold of the detail invariably fail. We become the bottleneck constraining the flow of fuel into the fire. Your ability to release the latent energy in your biggest resource – your people – is the key to your leadership effectiveness and impact. If we don't learn this key skill, we cause significant frustration and dissatisfaction to everyone around us. Taking the leap from finding comfort in the detail to managing people requires a completely different skillset and mindset.

This stage of our fire, and indeed our leadership maturity, requires us to focus on learning how to lead, as this is important for attracting and engaging brilliant people. The higher the quality of these employees (expertise, energy, talent), the more likely it is that growth can be sustained and purpose achieved. Our role is to provide purposeful, effective, visionary management of people and cash. It is about releasing the fuel, rather than controlling it. Quite simply, our fire will not grow unless we develop this vital skill. At best, we will be a fringe player; at worst, we will become irrelevant.

None of us is the finished product. We all have our own dysfunctional patterns, and often the problems we experience are of our own making. We get in our own way. Each of us has a core set of beliefs about how the world works. These beliefs are there for a good reason and have likely been learned throughout our childhood. The challenge is knowing that the beliefs that served us well as children may not serve us so well as adults. Let me share a few examples:

- Steve learned as a child that making peace between warring parents kept him safe. The result? As a manager he finds himself the peacemaker, avoids conflict at all costs and is unable to make unpopular (yet necessary) decisions.

- Harriet learned that excelling in school (A-grades, top of the class) won her mother's love. As a leader, she is a perfectionist, has high standards, is difficult to please – and is burning out.

- Vejay had a tough father who constantly belittled him. He learned never to show weakness, focusing on his internal world. As an adult, he is often passive-aggressive and his team call him 'the robot' due to his lack of emotion and authenticity.

- Deepak had an alcoholic father and learned to protect her siblings. As an adult, she takes responsibility for everything and everyone. Everyone loves her, but she has no life outside of work.

I could share hundreds of examples – many of them might trigger a, 'That's me' epiphany. My purpose here is to show that if we are not aware of how our unique history has shaped us as adults, and we are not actively engaged in self-growth and development, we not only limit ourselves, but also those we have responsibility for. The skills we learn through childhood in effect become our superpowers. The problem comes when we are unable to identify the point at which these same skills become our downfall.

In the Superman franchise owned by DC Comics, Kryptonite is a fictional material, often a green crystalline, originating from Superman's home planet of Krypton. It emits a unique, poisonous radiation that weakens and can kill Kryptonians. Kryptonite radiation can emit through any element except lead. Thus, Superman has a special lead suit to protect himself.

As leaders, we have to ensure that past traumas (we all have them) and the amazing coping mechanisms we learned as a child (our home planet) don't become our Kryptonite today. To protect ourselves and those we lead, we need the equivalent of Superman's lead suit: a continuous commitment to personal development, high levels of EQ and strong accountability.

Blindness to (or being aware of but not mitigating against) our Kryptonite (dysfunctional beliefs and behaviours) causes untold misery for those we lead, influence and impact. This is as true in our personal lives as it is in our professional ones.

If we have high EQ, we are likely aware of both our superpowers and our Kryptonite. But are we aware of how these weaknesses and strengths play out? Recognising that we are extremely caring is wonderful, but are we aware of where we take too much responsibility for others? In life, resilience is often beneficial, but do we carry on when we should stop? Can we be too friendly sometimes, blurring our relationships when we should maintain boundaries?

REFLECTIVE EXERCISE: Your superpowers/kryptonite

Think back and answer the following questions:

- What was top of your mind as you read this section?
- What are your key superpowers, and when do they become your Kryptonite? If it helps, consider the following list: confidence, courage, empathy, strength, drive, expertise, autonomy, intelligence, openness, resilience, friendliness, strategic thinking, operations, logical thinking, awareness.
- What is the impact of your superpowers on you? On others? And what's your development strategy?

If this is the first time you've explored these areas of your life, I encourage you to 'stay with it'. These are critical moments in your life as a wonderful human being and leader. The process of raising self-awareness can be both painful and hugely rewarding.

The keys to sustaining purposeful disruption

Sustaining purposeful disruption is difficult and certainly not for the faint hearted. To succeed, we need to be proactive in defining the kind of organisation we need to be. We need a particular type of leadership to shape culture and direction. Core to this endeavour is the quality of our thinking, aligned with how we learn. Argyris and Schön coined the phrase 'triple loop learning', which much like thinking about thinking, in this context, is learning about learning.[46] The triple loop framework is a mark of leadership maturity, and I will show you how you can apply it in your life and within your organisation. Within the original framework triple loop learning has three feedback loops – which I've adapted and call levels one, two and three.

Level One: Am I getting 'it' right?

Imagine you are successful in launching a new venture. Your fire attracts fuel and oxygen. As the venture grows, the challenge is to ensure your new staff are aligned with your vision, values and strategy. As the S-curve of growth (see figure below) shows, initial focus on sales and delivery moves on to ensuring consistent quality – essential in securing repeat orders and building long-term customer relationships. Finally, you need to maintain what you've built; this requires strong management practices, including policies, systems and processes.

Maintenance

Quality, Quality, Quality

Deliver, Deliver, Deliver

Sell, Sell, Sell

Your Fire

The S-curve of growth

Managers are brought in to effectively marshal and protect 'what is' (as compared to a leader's primary responsibility of focusing on 'what is to be'). Risks are easy to take when there is nothing to lose, but it's a different matter when one wrong decision can undo years of hard-fought gains.

But as highlighted in the excellent book *Lead and Disrupt*,[47] some companies get so good at management that they effectively sign their own death warrant. How? Their priority is managing the new status quo. Their thinking becomes dominated by, 'Are we getting it right?' If you're not careful, a new and powerful cartel is built over time to ensure everyone gets 'it' right. Seeking to protect what we have is basic human psychology, but in the context of disruption it's a deeply flawed approach that leads to a long, often slow, death – see figure below.

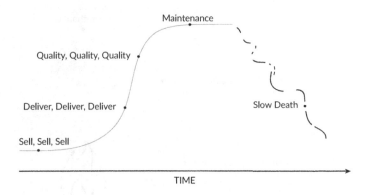

Maintenance

Quality, Quality, Quality

Deliver, Deliver, Deliver

Sell, Sell, Sell

Slow Death

TIME

S-curve of growth and death

What is at fault here is the quality of our thinking. Let me explain.

Look at any big business failure and you will find a history of Level One 'getting it right' thinking. They're inward-looking, dedicated to keeping the machine churning along. This was the case for Toys R Us, the big box store retailer that filed for Chapter 11 (US bankruptcy) in September 2017. Somehow, despite a name that suggests a magic adventure awaits, Toys R Us consistently failed to heed changes to the market-place and customer behaviour. Children were moving towards video games and didn't need to get their parents to take them to Toys R Us stores to buy them. Meanwhile, the shopping experience for physical toys had moved online. Despite this, Toys R Us stuck firmly to its big-box format, even though their stores were too big, jammed full of poorly merchandised inventory, and the customer service was terrible. It wouldn't have taken a huge amount of imagination or energy to disrupt this market – which, of course, is exactly what Amazon did, also transforming numerous other retail experiences. Other big box retailers, including Asda/Walmart and Costco, also dealt the chain some tough blows. I'm not equating Level One thinking with governance. As an organisation grows and matures, good-quality governance is a key determinant of long-term success. No one wants a nuclear power station to ignore rules, or rail companies to cut corners. Rather, I'm talking about the quality of thinking involved in different stages of leadership maturity.

At a personal level, engaging in safety-seeking behaviours is entirely natural. Without it, we would likely be dead. But if we are serious about solving big problems, we need to be aware of where safety seeking actively limits potential. Once we are aware, we need the courage to act.

Attending a meeting because it's in the calendar is an act of safety-seeking – speaking up and challenging might result in conflict, and conflict is dangerous. Across our organisations, each of us is guilty of prioritising emails over taking time to think; of not challenging a colleague on a decision for the sake of keeping the peace. It takes courage to think differently, boldness to speak up and energy to challenge the way things are done. To be disruptive, you have to disrupt. It starts with you.

When Level One thinking pervades an organisation, top to bottom, it ends up like Toys R Us. Or Blockbusters. Or Kodak. Innovation is stifled, agility killed and change resisted, all in the name of safety and control. What a travesty.

In their 'Seven transformations of leadership', David Rooke and William R Torbert explain how different leaders exhibit different kinds of action logic – ways in which they interpret their surroundings and react when their power or safety is challenged. When applied to Triple Level Learning, some 55% of leaders/managers operate with Level One thinking.[48] That's *over half* of all managers/leaders.

The key for those organisations seeking to disrupt their market continuously, is to ensure a culture of continuous *internal* disruption. To do so, we need to move beyond Level One thinking.

REFLECTIVE EXERCISE: Are you stuck on 'getting it right'?

Ask yourself honestly, what matters more as you look back at the end of a day or week?

- I'm up to date with my emails.
- My manager is happy with my progress.
- I've made demonstrable progress against a key strategic objective.

Level Two: Are we doing the right thing?

Where Level One provides a false sense of comfort (adherence to safety), Level Two causes discomfort. Here, we start to challenge what we believe about the world as we see it. Whether it's about our own thinking, or challenging others, the key question to ask is: what are the assumptions, principles or beliefs that drive your decisions and actions?

To answer, a degree of objectivity, or distance from the action itself is needed. What assumptions were Toys R Us operating under? It appears they were operating under the assumption that the chain was still the centre of the universe for the toy industry. No obvious attempt was made to counter the rise of more experience-based toy retailing, or to re-imagine the organisation in a more engaging and attractive way.

Challenging widely held assumptions does pay dividends and can, as UK-based pub chain JD Wetherspoon discovered, free an organisation up to focus on what matters. In 2018, stringent new EU GDPR data protection laws came into force and companies rushed to figure out how to get it right. This was a classic example of Level One learning and, to be fair, there was a good reason for it. Falling foul of the rules can result in fines of up to €20 million or 4% of an organisation's global turnover.[49] JD Wetherspoon, which has 852 outlets in 2022, asked a more powerful question: 'Are we doing the right things?'[50]

They had already experienced a data breach in 2015 and calculated that the risk of holding customer data was too great. As a result of asking this question, the company leadership decided to delete the entire customer email list, which contained an estimated 700,000 email addresses. Instead, they opted to rely on social media to engage with their customers. By asking a different question, they refined their approach and removed a risk in the process. (Or you could argue they played it safe and stuck to Level One thinking. What do you think?)

How can we actively move to Level Two thinking? Think about your humble kettle. Every morning, you fill it with water and turn it on. The coil heats and warms the water, until it reaches boiling temperature and switches off. At this point, all the water in the kettle is in the same energy state – at 100°C. Every H_2O molecule is uniformly vibrating with the same amount of energy. But as time passes, without the heat source, the water starts to cool and energy dissipates. At a molecular level, there is increasing variation in the energy states of each of the H_2O water molecules. Some still vibrate, others are stationary. The result is increasing molecular disorder, chaos and randomness. In physics, this process is known as entropy, and it applies to our organisations too. Returning to the fire analogy, we are talking about the dying embers of a once burning fire. Lukewarm, tepid, smoke but no heat…

Useful work is obtained from ordered molecular motion caused by the right amount of heat. The amount of entropy is also a measure of the molecular disorder, or randomness, of a system. An organisation can look safe, and even feel safe, but in reality, its heat is leaking out, resulting in increased disorder and tendency towards chaos. Sound familiar?

Large, inward-looking, defensive organisations run on autopilot. They are consumed by their rules, constantly looking at their own performance. Over time, they reach a bureaucratic state of entropy and slide towards chaos. How do we reverse entropy? By ensuring we gain constant energy from the outside. A learning organisation takes the time (T) to think critically and actively gains external energy (E):

$$T + E = \text{negentropy (the opposite of entropy)}$$

If you are serious about sustaining disruption, ensure that you, and your organisation, invest in E + T.

Some 40% of managers/leaders operate at Level Two thinking.[51] This level brings better insight, improved solutions and more effective outcomes than Level One.

If you are finding it difficult to manage the transition from Level One to Level Two, you might find the help of a consultant or coach advantageous. They will help you to think differently and to ask the right questions. They are well-positioned to assist you in looking outside of your situation and are more likely to see that to which you are blind. It's like walking into someone's house and noticing a smell to which the owner is oblivious. They will challenge your assumptions, question practices and turn principles on their head. Painful it might be, but what would Toys R Us and numerous other failed firms have given to have done things differently?

Level Two takes leaders beyond ticking boxes. It shifts the focus from 'getting it right' to asking deeper and more powerful questions. I always love the moment in coaching when I ask a question that shifts someone from Level One to Level Two thinking.

Typically, it might trigger a strong visceral reaction within the coachee. All of us operate in Level One because it's safe to do so – if we are ticking boxes, how can we possibly be getting it wrong?

The truth is, though Level Two thinking is clearly superior, it is also harder. It requires us to move out of our comfort zone, to let ourselves be uncomfortable. It is a journey that risks challenging everything we do, and that is never easy.

REFLECTIVE EXERCISE: Where is your thinking?

As a starting point to judge where you are, here are some questions to ask yourself:

- How much of my day-to-day meetings are concerned with Level One thinking?
- When was the last time you and your team booked time to challenge your assumptions proactively?
- How often do I/we think about the purpose behind what I/we do?
- How often do you ask for an external perspective (those not involved in your day-to-day) on your strategy?

Level Three: How do we decide what is right?

Level Three is concerned with global transformation and changing the way people think. It is practised by only a small fraction of leaders. Though I will mention some well-known and obvious examples, comparison is futile. I want to stress that any of us, with the right level of thinking, is able to disrupt in a profound way through this kind of thinking. What's more, in doing so we also disrupt ourselves. Coming back to the idea of the S-curve, Level Three thinking allows us to continuously create new S-curves before we enter the death spiral.

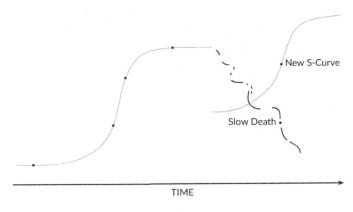

Building new S-curves

Elon Musk is an obvious example. He is thinking at a level that is way beyond where most others are, with not just one but a number of industry disruptors. He is the founder, CEO and chief engineer of SpaceX; angel investor, CEO and product architect of Tesla, Inc; founder of The Boring Company; co-founder of Neuralink and OpenAI; the president of Musk Foundation; and (as of April 2023), CEO of Twitter (owned by his company X Corp).

Another great example of someone in this category is the entrepreneur scientist Eric 'Astro' Teller. Teller is the CEO of Google X and the person responsible for figuring out how Google can disrupt successfully. He is referred to as the 'Captain of Moonshots', after the term for bringing magical, audacious ideas to life through science and technology.[52] How does Google achieve what they do? They rely on the maxim that true innovation happens when you try to improve something by ten times rather than by 10%. They call it '10x thinking'. While companies that focus on percentage improvements become more efficient, those that focus on 10x thinking are more likely to produce unicorns.

This third level is harder to explain, yet critical to achieving your purpose. It is where you, and those you work with, learn how to learn. Rather like thinking about thinking, this is how we figure out what is needed to allow us to learn better.

A good starting question that supports this type of learning/thinking is: 'How do we decide what's right?'

Roll that question around in your mind for a few moments. Or make it personal: 'How do I decide what's right?'

There is no one-word answer. There is no tick box. There is no binary yes/no, right/wrong answer. To answer properly, we need some time to think. It's not easy to think in this way, which is why many don't bother. It takes maturity. And time. The more complex the problem you are trying to solve, the more time you need.

It might sound counterintuitive, but sometimes we need to step away and take some time out to find the time we need. This is a strategy favoured by Microsoft founder Bill Gates, who goes away to his remote cottage with a bag full of books for a week at a time. He sets aside this time to get up to speed with the subjects he is interested in, to think and to devise a clear strategy. He's not just thinking about Microsoft.[53] Some of the projects the Bill and Melinda Gates Foundation are working on are trying to eradicate polio and malaria, create clean energy and provide clean water to all – all ambitious and disruptive targets. Time for quiet, measured reflection is required.

REFLECTIVE EXERCISE: Practising Level Three thinking

Book some time in your calendar to get started on breaking down your problems by asking yourself the following questions:

- What are we trying to achieve?
- Why are we trying to achieve it?
- What are the important values that underpin the what, the why and the how?
- What have we learned from previous projects that we can apply here?
- What are the questions we need to ask, and how can we improve them?

Expanding upon the exercise above, it may also help to break your answers down in terms of the specifics of your purpose. Many organisations list integrity (or a variant thereof) as one of their core values. Yet in reality, how many boards have asked themselves: 'How can we improve integrity within our board meetings, or in our conversations with our stakeholders, or in our engagement with our customers?' Integrity is more than a word on a wall. It means much more than simply telling the truth. Integrity demands a congruence between thought and deed. It is visible where there are strong values and principles and a lack of hypocrisy. It is utterly trustworthy and demands your true, authentic, genuine, self, in all contexts. When seen in this light, integrity becomes difficult to achieve. It requires wrestling with hard questions, and often imprecise answers. Organisations that list integrity as key to their purpose are well-intentioned, but if they lack follow-through they are utterly hypocritical.

REFLECTIVE EXERCISE: Finding integrity

To ensure you are leading with integrity, consider the following:

- Within your work context, what two or three powerful questions could you be asking yourself/ your team related to your integrity?
- How can you improve these questions?
- How can you better support and embed your purpose deep within the DNA of your organisation?
- What's required to help you get better answers?

A leader who asks the difficult, but right, questions, and takes time to figure out the answers, is one who is likely to successfully challenge the status quo. It may be uncomfortable, but it creates the foundation for disruptive growth.

Around 5% of leaders operate at Level Three thinking,[54] divided between 'strategists' (4%) and 'alchemists' (1%). A strategist is someone who 'generates organisational and personal transformations,' exercising 'the power of mutual inquiry, vigilance and vulnerability for both the short and long term.' The alchemists, making up just 1% of the leadership population, 'generate social transformations.' They 'integrate material, spiritual and societal transformation.' This is where true societal disruption takes place, most often for the betterment of society. We need that in today's global climate.

One of the most important characteristics of Level Three leaders is not just how they choose to spend their existing resources of energy and time (E+T) in the most focused way, but also how they *gain* energy and time. As such, it's important to review your energy and time requirements frequently. The path to success is to ensure that the hours you put in are meaningful and purposeful. It is critical to step off the rollercoaster. To step out of the storm. If you can grasp this principle and apply it daily within your life, prepare to achieve the seemingly impossible.

At the simplest level, we all have the capacity to gain time by removing a couple of meetings from our diary. (Try it, it is remarkably easy.) Now, you have two hours you didn't have before – a chance to think about bigger things. It's so simple and basic, but we all seem to struggle with it. You can take this further by taking advantage of two key things:

1. External energy (E)
2. Time to think (T)

External energy and time to think

In the 1998 film The Truman Show, Jim Carrey stars as Truman Burbank, an upbeat twenty-nine-year-old insurance salesman. As he goes about his life, he is unaware that he is in fact a reality TV star. Five thousand hidden cameras capture every aspect of his life within a carefully constructed film set. His wife, family and friends are all paid actors. It's only when he listens to voices outside the closed system of the film set that he starts asking the right questions. The producers (the status quo, acting as a powerful cartel) resisted his every move, and for obvious reasons – he was their livelihood, the central character of their production, their cash cow. But by giving his attention to the right things he was able to break free.

Unless we seek to be like Truman, stuck in a world of our own making, we must be open to new perspectives, thoughts and energy. We need an external perspective, otherwise we just engage with the same people and do the same things over and over.

Taking time to think is invaluable, yet today there are more and more distractions that prevent us from doing so. The advent of mobile technology has been a brilliant asset, but it has also conspired to steal those precious moments of self-reflection. We are all guilty. I know I am. Whether it is checking status updates while on the toilet, catching up on the latest news on a commute, listening to music and podcasts while driving or checking for likes while eating. When you are absorbed by these things, you miss out on the time to consider your best ideas.

I believe that the brilliant theoretical physicist Stephen Hawking provided so much new insight and thinking (at least in part) because his body was ravaged by early-onset motor neurone disease. It robbed him of his physical abilities. Yet, by being forced into his mind, he was able to think deeply and for long periods of time. We understand much more about the mysteries of the universe as a result. There are numerous other examples of great thinkers who positively shaped our culture, faith, morals, laws and trade, because they were proactive and took time to think. By 'thinking', here, I mean spending regular, significant and dedicated hours on this task. Aristotle, Plato, Newton and Michelangelo spent their days thinking, and all of them disrupted the world. Similarly, the founders of the world's main religions devoted time to developing the mind through reflection, prayer and meditation.

There are numerous examples of disruptive business leaders who have figured this out. The founder of fashion brand Superdry, Julian Dunkerton, whose net worth is some £440m, carries an old, cheap non-smartphone, the Nokia 6310, which can only make and receive calls and send texts. Why? 'My brain is probably freer to comprehend what is actually happening around me and make better decisions because it is not clogged with rubbish,' he says.[55] He has a good point. Anything that demands our attention removes our time to think.

There is not much that can't be solved by taking a break from it and focusing on something else. It releases our incredible minds and gives them a chance to explore the possibilities. In a TED Talk, Tim Harford talks about the importance of the 'slow motion multitask'.[56] He explains how great thinkers, inventors and disruptors such as Albert Einstein, Charles Darwin, Twyla Tharp and Michael Crichton worked on multiple projects over a long time. When they ran into a brick wall on one project, they would turn their focus to another, sometimes over a period of many years. Solutions presented themselves when they were not focusing on the wall they had hit.

Sir Richard Branson, who we talked about earlier, has written and spoken many times about what it takes to be successful. He talks of dreaming big, being bold and, critically, taking time out. He encourages us to schedule time just to dream and allow our minds to wander. 'Far too many people get weighed down in doing, and never take the time to think and feel,' he says.[57] When at work, Branson deliberately drinks twenty cups of tea because, he says, it gives him a moment to stop and think without being distracted, and that, often, this time sparks new ideas as his mind wanders, or helps him find solutions to problems that have been bugging him.[58]

REFLECTIVE EXERCISE: Energy

Try and identify where you get your energy from.
For inspiration, it might be:

- Holidays
- Exercise
- Time to prepare
- Rest/doing nothing
- Time with family/friends
- Meditation/prayer
- Nature
- Conferences/seminars
- Working with a coach/mentor
- Development programmes
- Hobbies
- Strategy/blue sky days
- Walking
- Networking
- Speaking with customers, suppliers or partners
- Meeting industry leaders/peers
- Taking a lunch hour

Now ask yourself the following questions:

- Are you prioritising those areas that give you external energy?
- How much time are you taking per week, or per day, just to think?
- How much time do you spend talking to people (customers, prospects, competitors, employees) to gain external energy/alternative perspectives?

- When was the last time (other than a holiday) you allowed yourself to be bored?

Finally, choose and prioritise one thing that gives you energy, and spend a minimum of fifteen minutes doing that thing within the next twenty-four hours.

If your first reaction is 'Don't you realise how busy I am?', I hear you! Taking time out to think is a proactive decision. It doesn't happen by itself. The truth is, the more senior you are, the greater the demands on your time. At this level, investing just an hour in seeking external energy and perspectives can bring insight that changes your whole approach.

It's a key reason why we set up WeQual Global, a global community of leaders representing every sector, job function and culture.[59] Through regular virtual sixty-minute sessions members gain outside–in global best-practice perspectives and development support on leadership and critical business issues. Feedback is consistently high – Net Promoter Score (NPS) of 9.5+ – with participants reporting they feel more 'connected', 'reflective', 'challenged' and, my personal favourite, 'energised'.

Other ways to gain that all-important external energy include making appointments to see your most important customer, supplier or business partner. Seek out a mentor – this is often as easy as sending them a short LinkedIn request: 'Hi, Jo, I love what you've done in your career. It would be great to meet for a fifteen-minute coffee and get your advice.' What's the worst that can happen? Reach out to someone who does a similar or different role in another company (and please don't let any sense of imposter syndrome get in the way). When you meet, talk candidly about your biggest challenge. Be vulnerable. Ask for their insight. Ask them about their challenges, too. What have they learned? How might it apply to your own situation? I guarantee that not only will you build stronger relationships, but you will also gain fresh insight that can power more impactful decisions.

Apply this same approach to seeking out peers in other sectors. Attend conferences, both within and outside of your industry. Get up to date with the latest research in your field. Take a few hours to read about the latest technology. Read something about history. Stay open to personal learning and development. Do something challenging.

REFLECTIVE EXERCISE: Impacting your team

This section has focused on your own personal energy and time (E+T). Now think about the impact on those you lead. As a manager or leader, you set the tone. Take a few minutes to think about how you can support them with their own E+T. Here are some ideas:

Think about what has stood out to you from this book so far, and introduce it as an agenda item for an upcoming team meeting. Put time in your diary before the meeting to prepare.

- Challenge your team regarding the number of meetings they attend. Which are a waste of their time? Where can they empower/delegate? Get each team member to name one meeting they will no longer attend. Encourage them to reallocate that time strategically (on E+T).

- Plan a half-day session for your team to explore something new. If you are struggling for a topic, invite someone from outside your normal environment to introduce a new topic, challenge your thinking and/or facilitate discussion.

- Bring together a small multi-disciplined team from different parts of the business to find solutions to a pressing issue. Encourage quality time and divergent thinking.

- Building on the multi-disciplined team, invite a key stakeholder not normally involved in problem-solving (eg, an important customer, supplier, union rep or investor/shareholder).

- Take your team away to an off-site event designed to challenge thinking.

It is important that you act now (instruct your EA/team, send email invitations, set diary time to action, etc).

Think like a leader

To close this chapter, I'd like to offer a few thoughts on how to think – or, perhaps, how not to think.

Thinking is something we've all done all our lives, but *productive* thinking is a skill. When we are under stress, the survival part of our brain kicks in (mainly the amygdala) and our focus narrows. Below, I have listed some unhelpful and unproductive thinking patterns. You may recognise a few of them:

- **All-or-nothing thinking:** Everything becomes polarised in one camp or another. It is right or wrong, with no grey areas in between. 'I'm a total success,' or 'I'm a total failure.' 'I can have it all,' or 'I'll get nothing.' 'It will be fantastic,' or 'It'll be a complete disaster.'

- **Catastrophising:** You are 100% convinced that the absolute worst is going to happen, whatever you do. This type of thinking is also known as fortune-telling, as you try to predict the (negative) future of your business/project without considering other, more likely outcomes.

- **Emotional reasoning:** Against all available evidence, you reason something must be true because your gut instinct is telling you so. 'I'm right, I can feel it.'

- **Labelling:** Once again ignoring the available evidence, a leader assigns themselves or someone else a specific label: 'They're a loser. They'll never be able to see this through.'

- **Mental filter:** A mental filter is applied, obliterating one aspect of the whole picture, with judgements based on that small issue. 'X didn't work, so I/we won't be able to succeed with Y.'

- **Mind reading:** A conviction about what others are thinking and/or what is motivating them without considering other, more likely possibilities. 'They think I don't know what I'm doing.'

- **Over-generalisation:** Sweeping statements that assume that because one thing happened, another will surely follow. 'We are market leaders in one product area, so launching a new product will double our income.' 'We failed in the last product launch, so we won't launch another product.'

- **Personalisation:** Everything is about you, good or bad. Others are performing badly to frustrate you, even though there are other more plausible explanations for their lack of output. 'We won that deal because of me,' or, 'Mary cost me that sale because she didn't complete the project on time.'

- **'Should' and 'must' statements:** A precise, fixed and unshakeable belief about how you or others should behave. This leads on to an over-estimation of how badly things will turn out if these expectations are not met. 'The sales director *should* see our top ten customers monthly, or we will lose them,' or, 'Our employees *must* be in the office to work on the right things.'

- **Tunnel vision:** The negative aspects of a situation are all that present themselves, to the exclusion of all other factors, including the positive ones. 'Numbers are down, we've lost our key engineer, we're doomed,' despite the fact that a new service is growing exponentially.

REFLECTIVE EXERCISE: Thinking errors

Think about the following questions:

* Which thinking error do you engage in the most often?
* What can you do to try and rectify this?

Suggestion: speak to a boss, colleague or direct report about your tendency, and ask them to tell you when they notice you doing this.

Each of us engages in common thinking errors, and most of the time we are completely unaware we're doing it. These errors often show up in Level One thinking, ie, constrained or limited thinking. Awareness is what makes the difference – examining our thinking (against the list above), or by being curious and open when discussing our beliefs with others, can be enough to help us think differently. As cognitive behavioural psychology has demonstrated, if we can change how we think, we change how we behave.

Another way to change how you think is by accessing the creative and analytical parts of your brain. Both parts are required to weigh all the different possible options, question our assumptions and consider new and creative ways around any roadblocks. One of the best ways to do this is to 'train' your brain through meditation. While some may baulk at the 'alternative' nature of the idea, it has some high-profile advocates in the business world. Steve Jobs was an early adopter of meditation and said it helped him think clearly and be more in the present: 'Your mind just slows down, and you see a tremendous expanse in the moment. You see so much more than you could see before.'[60]

At the simplest level, allocate some time away from your screens. You may not be willing to follow Julian Dunkerton's lead and switch to a non-smartphone, but what about starting the day with a few minutes of meditation, rather than immediately checking up on emails and the news?

There is no one way to meditate. The idea is to quieten your mind for a period of time. Doing so reconnects us to ourselves and brings us a sense of peace.[61] Likely outcomes are more energy, fresh insight and increased resilience. US Zen Master Shunryu Suzuki calls it 'beginner's mind'.[62] This is where your thoughts quieten and your mind opens up to see the present reality. It helps you step away from common thinking patterns and be less judgemental.

In the below exercise I suggest one way to get started, but if it doesn't work for you, find something that does. There are squillions of books, videos and articles on the subject. There are also guided meditation apps, which will require you going back to your smartphone, but for the right reasons.

REFLECTIVE EXERCISE: Try meditation

Set a timer for the period you wish to meditate for – start with five minutes and increase to fifteen. Sitting or lying comfortably, pick a sound and concentrate on it. It might be your breathing, an air conditioning unit or fan, distant traffic or bird song. I have downloaded the sound of a waterfall onto my phone, which I play on repeat. Others use rainfall, white noise or binaural beats.

Try to focus on that sound to the exclusion of everything else. As you do so, your mind is likely to wander to pressing issues. That's OK. Note the issue, let the thought go and refocus on the sound. Each time your mind wanders, bring it back without judgement. You will be reminded of lots of important things, and you will be tempted to jump up and action them. Resist. Refocus your mind on the sound to the exclusion of all else. At the end of your session, note how you feel.

If you can manage even a minute without thinking about something, congratulate yourself. The more you practise, the better you will become and the longer you will be able to meditate for. Aim to reach 15 minutes a day. The results will be self-evident.

Managing energy and time is the secret to your long-term success. The more senior you are, the more imperative it is that you take control. Being busy is a drug. Being wanted and needed provides a great high. But true disruption requires an ongoing commitment to E+T that will pay dividends.

Let me share a story of a CEO I once coached. She had a need to disrupt her market but was clearly run ragged trying to do everything without pausing to think where she should best spend her time. After much discussion, she agreed to take a day a month out of the office – on work time. When we spoke later, she had an entirely different outlook: 'I had no idea that taking time out like that could be in the best interests of the company,' she said. She went on to successfully disrupt the area her company was focusing on, with a hugely positive outcome.

If I said to you that you can increase the effectiveness of your leadership and disruption if you freed up a day a month, what would you say? 'Impossible. I don't have time. I have too much to do. You don't understand the pressure I'm under.'

This was the response of the world's largest delivery company, Just Eat Takeaway.com's group finance director and executive committee member, Tom Pereira. During the pandemic, the company had grown exponentially and the Dutch Takeaway.com acquired Just Eat PLC in a share acquisition, and then acquired America's Grubhub. The result was an organisation that grew from 3,600 employees in 2018 to 13,780 at the time of printing (plus hundreds of thousands of delivery drivers).[63] When I spoke to him, Tom was wrestling with the complex challenges of defining the new financial structures and operating models required to enable the company to succeed. He had a young family and was working every possible hour. It was clear he needed time to think. I challenged him to 'free up half a day a week for the next three weeks to think.' His initial response was to say that was impossible. If you think coaching is wishy-washy, think again. Tom was under enormous pressure, and I challenged him hard. He managed to free up the time – and realised he needed far more.

A year later, I interviewed him as part of a leadership development programme we were delivering with 130 of his company's top leaders. He told me, 'I now try to keep one day free a week to think – or at least to focus on the strategic challenges.' A short while later, within one of the newly formed ExCo meetings, one of the other C-suite members said, 'Tom is the one who is the most thoughtful and provides the clearest thinking on how we should structure the company.' Taking time out to think matters.

Changing mindset (our thoughts and beliefs) is difficult. This is why coaching and development are so important. The truth is, you are in charge, regardless of seniority. You own your calendar. Stop thinking that you need to be available to everyone and that you need to answer every email, or continually demonstrate your worth, or attend every meeting. Give yourself time to breathe – and think.

Your biggest responsibility is to lead effectively. To do that, you need to take control of your energy and time. Making time to think, really think, releases your full potential and will stand you in good stead for your next stage of growth. Without it, you risk staying stuck just like Truman. What are you missing out on by not devoting quality time to thinking?

REFLECTIVE EXERCISE: Making time to think

Make a few notes on the following:

- When was the last time you gave your mind a break?
- Do you meditate? What do you gain from doing so? Based on your experience, what outcomes would you gain from spending a few more minutes on this each day?
- Do you allocate time each week just to think?
- Can you add three hours a month of pure thinking time to your calendar?

6
Continuous Personal Development

I worked with an impressive senior vice president at a global company. Everyone on Sonia's (name changed) team, from her direct reports to the CFO she reported into, loved her and thought she was doing a brilliant job. I knew this first-hand because I had interviewed them all. Yet Sonia was wracked with self-doubt. English was her second language and she felt perpetually self-conscious about her accent. She'd also convinced herself that she wasn't achieving all she needed to.

We spoke around the time of her annual review and Sonia was clearly more anxious than usual. In the particular multinational she worked for, each person's review was conducted by a manager once removed, so in Sonia's case, the job fell to the CEO. The CEO was much admired and respected throughout the company and the darling of investors. He had a well-earned reputation as an inspirational visionary who had done fantastic things for the company, having transformed its fortunes over previous years. Sonia had been asked to put together a one-page overview in preparation for the meeting.

We met prior to the meeting and she'd already put together her first draft. I read it and could see straight away that there was a problem. She'd come at it from the angle of predicting what hoops she needed to jump through to impress her CEO. She'd filled the page with her qualifications and previous roles, her current roles and responsibilities, and trotted out the same buzzwords the CEO was fond of using. It's as if her entire approach centred around, 'What could I say that will resonate and impress?'

It was the wrong approach. Sonia had fallen into the trap that many people do of trying to please her boss while simultaneously communicating her own unconscious biases about herself. 'I'm not good enough.' In a bid to change her perspective, I asked her a simple question:

'Imagine you are meeting with one of your team and you've asked them for a one pager of what they want to do. What would you say to them?'

'I would want them to tell me precisely what they want, so I could help them,' she replied. 'I want to see them succeed, develop and grow.' I repeated back what she'd said. 'You'd want them to tell you precisely what they want, so you could help them. You want to see them succeed, develop and grow?'

'Yes, of course,' she confirmed. I waited for the penny to drop...

'And what do you think your CEO wants?' And there it was. The 'aha' moment.

Sonia is not alone. Without realising it, most of us are most likely unconsciously engaging in similar behaviours on a daily basis. Sonia was approaching the situation as if the CEO had all the power and she had none. The psychological framework of transactional analysis (TA) describes this scenario well.[64] Sonia had moved into the ego state of a child, and placed the CEO firmly into the role of parent. 'He has the power, and I have to try and impress him.'

Transactional analysis

Within TA, there are three ego states: parent, adult and child. These can be described as follows:

- A parent can be nurturing or controlling/critical.

- A child can be compliant, rebellious, or playful and acts based on emotions and feelings.

- The adult state is one where we are non-judgemental, open-minded, interested, confident and grounded in reality.

Ideally, we stay in a balanced adult state, inviting adult-to-adult relationships and, where appropriate, draw upon appropriate parent or child behaviours.

Parent-to-child or child-to-parent relationships can be sustained over the long term, but there are always downsides. Parent-to-parent – especially where this is critical-to-critical – usually results in heated arguments, relationship breakdowns and even all-out hostility. When two nurturing parents relate, they try to outdo each other in their care and support. Child-to-child adult relationships are typically characterised by strong emotions, impulsiveness and demands that personal needs are met. When we engage in these child behaviours, it's typically driven by childhood traumas and unmet needs.

At the outset of our careers, we might find ourselves in child mode – seeking to please our manager – and for good reason. We don't know what we are doing, and we need our monthly salary. Though this aim-to-please approach might work early in our careers, it becomes less effective as our responsibilities increase. Looking for validation is a trap because it stops us from being our true selves. We check our behaviours, what we desire and what we say in the pursuit of being liked. We expend energy and time looking for approval outside of ourselves. This stops us from disagreeing with others, taking the initiative and taking bold risks. Approval-seekers rarely disrupt.

In much of the world, workplace encounters need to be adult-to-adult regardless of the hierarchical relationship, and whatever the cultural historical norms.[65] This does not mean there will never be conflict – far from it. But the conflict is about how to achieve a goal, rather than rooted in a need to protect egos.

We have already seen the danger of entering a conversation with a CEO with the mindset of a compliant child. If this happens, the best result we could hope for is that the CEO changes the dynamic and invites an adult-to-adult conversation. But wouldn't it be better to enter that conversation as an adult right from the start?

Think of investor pitches, interviews, sales meetings, meetings with a mentor or coach, a performance review or being asked to provide help. Each is an example where it is easy to fall into the trap of initiating a parent-to-child or child-to-parent relationship. Though it can be difficult, and you might require the support of a coach to get there, adult-to-adult is where you will drive the best results.

REFLECTIVE EXERCISE: Child, adult or parent?

Think back to some key interactions in the last week and choose the number below that best captures your dominant thinking, words or behaviours:

1. I think you are an idiot, but I smile sweetly, listen and do what you ask me to do.
2. I bend the rules, and seek to challenge to bring some excitement.
3. I know best and use words like 'should', 'must' and 'need' a lot.
4. I'd rather be hit by a bus than do what they are telling me to do.
5. I'm open to new information – what's required to move forward?

6. How can I help you? How do you feel? What do you need?

Now check your answer to see what it might imply about your ego state:

Answers: 1, compliant child; 2, playful child; 3, critical parent; 4, rebellious child; 5, adult; 6, nurturing parent.

Consider, what is your default ego state when interacting with others? Do you adopt a parent or a child role? What roles do you adopt in different scenarios?

Being aware of how we approach interactions can make a big difference to outcomes. In the case of Sonia, she changed the way she tackled her presentation and spoke to her CEO, adopting an adult stance. She summarised her main achievements to date, highlighted some key strategic directions she felt would support the company and its stated objectives and outlined why she was the right person to lead those programmes. The outcome? The CEO took notes ('He never takes notes, Mark,' she later told me), the meeting overran by thirty minutes and he gave her the green light to proceed with some exciting disruptive global projects. Two years and a new CEO later, Sonia has now taken a new global role to drive organisational culture and effectiveness. Knowing her as I do, I'm sure there's even more to come.

In the same way we don't want to turn up as a child, neither do we want to take on the parent role when working with colleagues. I remember the first major leadership development programme that I won at a company called CDA, a manufacturer of kitchen appliances. As I was driving to facilitate the first session just outside Nottingham, UK, I reflected on the company and my role. I'd spent some considerable time with Ian Kershaw, then founder and CEO, and his board and had carried out several interviews with the senior managers. I considered that I had a good handle on the issues and what was needed. As I drove through rolling fields, I considered my own journey and what I'd learned about myself. I realised I was very much in parent mode: I was going to show/tell them how to be better managers. Doing so would push all these wonderful managers into child mode (compliant, playful and/or rebellious). How utterly arrogant of me. I was firmly in the, 'I'm OK, you're *not* okay' parent role. The thought was abhorrent to me and I quickly reminded myself of my flaws and the managers' brilliance. Before I entered their offices I was back in the 'I'm okay, you're okay' adult-to-adult space. I vowed to always check in with myself before any professional interaction: how do I see myself, and how do I see the other?

Awareness is key in all our interactions as a leader. Most (good) bosses don't want to take the role of parent when interacting with an employee. They want to speak adult-to-adult with their colleagues, since this is the most effective and constructive form of communication. It should be said, this works the other way around too. An incompetent leader may adopt a confrontational, critical parent stance, strongly encouraging their reports into adult-compliant child roles. This results in sycophantic followers who never dare to challenge the often overly confident leader who is convinced they are right, even as the company hits the rocks. We saw earlier in the section on narcissistic leadership how this can look in practice.

What do we do if our boss behaves as a critical parent? Do we assume the child role to keep the peace and maintain a dysfunctional yet harmonious relationship? The answer depends on what you want. If you want to disrupt positively, you need to figure out how to change the relationship dynamic to adult-to-adult.

If you find yourself working for a critical parent leader, or within a critical parent culture, and you've not been able to change the dynamic no matter what you've tried, you may want to consider leaving for an organisation that values and practises collaborative adult relationships in the pursuit of achieving meaningful purpose. I promise you, there are many who would welcome your expertise and approach.

Each of us holds a complex set of beliefs derived from our unique childhood experiences, and these beliefs drive our behaviours, whether we are aware of them or not. Many serve us well, especially where parental love was unconditional (freely given without the requirement to receive anything in return). However, many don't.

Revisiting the superpower/Kryptonite theme, the key to being well-rounded adults, and leaders, is:

1. Being aware of how beliefs and behaviours impact ourselves, and those we live and work with.

2. Recognising when those same beliefs and behaviours are no longer serving us.

3. Putting in the hard work of changing our beliefs to engage in behaviours that better serve us as adults.

Feedback

Feedback from a colleague might sting your ego but research shows that even the most critical feedback can support our development. Painful things said during a relationship breakup can cause us to reflect deeply. Negative feedback from investors or market analysts, being passed over for that desired promotion or not winning a big deal are powerful opportunities to learn more about ourselves. It is difficult to let go of beliefs and behaviours that no longer serve us. But remember: what has got you here won't get you there. What is it you need to change to take the next step?

WeQual runs three annual award ceremonies for outstanding female leaders ready for a future C-suite executive committee role (The Americas, APAC, EMEA). The awards process includes an interview between the VP and a CEO or chair from a global company – recent interviewers include the CEOs of Mondi, Anglo American, Rolls-Royce, Schneider Electric, Wipro, Sanofi, Kellogg's, HCL Technologies, Cipla, the vice chair of Mastercard and chair of Barclays UK. We ask for notes from the interview and then provide one-to-one feedback to the women.

Most of it is extremely positive – they are, after all, outstanding leaders – but occasionally the feedback can also be cutting:

- 'She talks too much.'
- 'She came across as cold.'
- 'She lacked vision.'

Katie, the founder of WeQual, and I have had many conversations on how best to deliver feedback in a positive way, but we are unanimous in our agreement that we should not try to sugar-coat it. It's a constant surprise how often these senior leaders are incredibly grateful for honest and direct feedback. 'Who else would say this to me?' they ask.

A receptive attitude to feedback, however difficult it is to hear, is a hallmark of great leadership. If we want to change the things about ourselves that are detrimental to us and our leadership, we have to be prepared for negative feedback. When was the last time you asked for feedback *knowing* it would be critical?

Changing a core belief about ourselves can be incredibly powerful. I remember coaching Abu Bundu-Kamara, a senior director at Expedia Group. When we spoke, Abu said he was exhausted by having to constantly prove himself: 'I feel like everyone's eyes are on me all the time, waiting for me to get it wrong.'

I asked him how he knew that to be true. As a coach, I'm often aware that asking tough questions can be perceived as lacking in empathy. I understood some of Abu's history. He had been the only black kid in an all-white school. Early in his career, he had been the only black man in his department. It was difficult for him not to feel different. But, in his current context, how did he *know* that everyone was waiting for him to fail?

'What would it look like if, when you walked into a room, you felt like an equal and that everyone wanted you to succeed?' I asked him.

Abu had never looked at it from this viewpoint and, when he did, he found it liberating. Based on his past experience, he'd been entering every situation with a child ego, convinced everyone was looking down on him, waiting for him to make a mistake. For much of his life, that was his lived experience, so he had every right to take this approach. His unique history had taught him to think like that. It had served him well, as he had proven himself time and time again. And yet, was this belief serving him in his current situation? Was what had got him here going to get him *there*?

When we dug deeper, it turned out that he had an inspirational manager who was also black. She'd been encouraging and supportive from the off. This didn't sound like someone who wanted him to fail.

'What difference would it make if you were able to change what you *think* others are thinking, and assume that in fact they want you to succeed?' I pressed. Abu smiled excitedly and agreed that his life would look very different. My heart went out to him. I do not know what it is like to be him. But I do know that, free from the fear of what others think, he will be happier and more fulfilled, better able to realise his purpose. (I met up with Abu again very recently, and I was humbled as he told me how this conversation changed his life.)

REFLECTIVE EXERCISE: Key takeaways from part two

We covered a lot in this last section. What stood out to you?

Some questions to consider:

- Are you aware of when you move between adult, parent and child modes? How aware are you of the impact of your ego state on others?

- What did your upbringing teach you about yourself? What is it you need to do to gain acceptance? Is the approval of others important to you? Where does this stop you from making difficult decisions?

PART THREE
ACCELERATING DISRUPTION

7

Increasing Fuel – Growing Your Talent Base

Once a fire is burning, the type and quantity of fuel used to sustain it is key to its growth and longevity. In an organisational context, this means attracting and engaging with ever-increasing quantities of talent and cash.

However, one of the biggest threats to increasing fuel is the internal status quo. The board, leaders and culture seek to protect what is (Level One thinking), rather than seeking heat-generating collisions necessary for Level Two and Three disruption. Structure and culture begin to act like chains, restricting you to the existing way of doing things. Rules, systems and processes force people to think the same, behave the same and even collude to maintain a false peace. Before long, total uniformity rules. Everyone acts the same way and the blanket of fabricated agreement smothers the fire. No one dares speak up, challenge or do things differently. When an organisation reaches this stage, you can forget about disruption. It may not even survive. But how does it get there to start with?

Reed Hastings, the founder of Netflix, has written eloquently about this in *No Rules Rules: Netflix and the culture of reinvention*.[66] He speaks about how, as his first startup, PureSoftware, grew, the processes and policies that were brought in one after another stifled the creativity that had initially fuelled the firm's growth. Good people left to find more flexible and less rule-bound regimes that would allow their innovative spirit to flourish. Bogged down by process, the firm stagnated. PureSoftware was eventually sold to a larger competitor.

At his next startup Hastings vowed to prioritise flexibility, employee freedom and innovation, rather than error prevention and rule adherence. The result was captured in the famous culture deck of that next firm, Netflix, which has been shared online by millions of businesspeople worldwide. As the title of his book suggests, he argues that the key to success is setting as few rules as possible. The way to affect this is to build an organisation stuffed with high performers. The greater the talent, the more freedoms you can offer and, therefore, fewer rules are required. Ultimately, it is the quality of leadership that enables, empowers and releases the potential of high performers. Building psychologically safe workplaces where people can thrive requires talented and well-developed leaders.

Sometimes, shaking a company out of the torpor of the internal status quo may involve a complete change of direction, or even an entirely new environment. This was the experience of Jean-Pascal Tricoire, who became CEO of Schneider Electric in 2006 (with over 135,000 employees in 2022), having previously held various positions in the company based in France, Italy, China and South Africa. Upon taking the top job, Jean-Pascal noted that the company had a 'miss' in Asia, where 'the core growth of urbanisation, of manufacturing, of the population and, therefore, digitisation, was not happening where we were at that time.' He told me:

'I inherited a company that was more like a federation of different companies. Our customers wanted us to solve their problems, but we couldn't do that with one element of that federation at a time. There were two ways of solving this. We could restructure or make the company totally different. So we turned the company upside down, eliminated a lot of individual units and created an entirely new vision, based on a digital architecture (supplying digital systems and solutions), which was something the company had not done before.

'Making that change was a big moment and it required a lot of adaptation. The people who worked in the individual parts of the business

were entrepreneurial and accountable,
but I needed them to change their state
of mind. They had to be entrepreneurial and
accountable but on a much larger scale.'

Over the next few years, Jean-Pascal scattered his
entire leadership team across the globe – to other
parts of Europe, North America, the Middle East and
Asia. He himself moved to Hong Kong from Paris, the
historic headquarters of the 180-year-old company.
Explaining this decision, he said:

'We needed to act like a global business and
that meant, in part, making a physical change.
I realised this when I was building the Asian
business. Initially, I was doing it all from Paris,
which was comfortable. But I didn't want it
to be comfortable. My priority was speed and
transformation: I wanted to move away from
a mindset of centralised operations. I moved
to Hong Kong and moved the senior team to
where they needed to be, in multiple parts of
the world.'

Jean-Pascal concedes that this upheaval may seem like
a difficult choice and that, to begin with, not everyone on the team thought it was a great idea. However,
he added that with preparation and an agile mindset,
it can go smoothly. The majority of the team wanted
to make the change and were excited about the new,
more efficient digital infrastructure. Despite the early

pushback not a single senior colleague left the company. Talking about this mindset, he said:

'My preferred sport is white water kayaking. I know that you need a strong sense of direction if you want to survive the rapids, I know also that waves never happen as forecasted, so you need agility to adapt. All of the team has to get through, but all of them will meet different conditions and will have to make their own decisions. I don't believe that to be in charge of a company you have to micromanage every step made by every person. The most important thing is to fix a strong direction, choose the right team players and help each other out as unexpected conditions unfold. We empower people to make the most of their energy and resources.'

Decentralising the team encouraged greater innovation and creativity at Schneider Electric. It also created a meritocracy, since everyone on the senior team has the opportunity to rise to the highest position in the company, wherever their location.

It would have been easy for Jean-Pascal not to have moved his team around the world, and for him to have remained in Paris. It was, after all, a French company. But he didn't. Leading disruption is not easy, and it is incumbent on us as leaders to lead by example. How can we ask others to go where we will not?

REFLECTIVE EXERCISE: Decision-making

Think about some decisions you have made in the past or recently. Which of them have results?

Is there a key decision waiting to be made that has the potential to transform future results?

The need for diversity

No one likes corporate buzzwords, and 'diversity' is one at the top of the list that gets people's eyes rolling. Yet it's important.

Winnie is a short-haired, 5-foot-tall, middle-aged, black woman.[67] Winnie is burning with purpose and takes no prisoners. Her tumultuous background includes walking across Europe from Ethiopia as a young girl. At twelve, she watched her father die at the hands of a mob. She fended off gangs and protected her younger siblings while her mother worked four jobs to keep the family together. Her life experiences have forged in her a strength of character that belies her slight frame. She is driven to be at the top of her game. She is on a mission, with fire in her belly. She has read every book, is *au fait* with the latest research, attends conferences and listens to every TED Talk. When she speaks, she still has a distinct accent but is happy to converse in French or English. She got her PhD by studying in the evenings and at weekends.

By sheer force of will and a lot of hard work, Winnie has risen to the top ranks of a blue-chip firm. Even so, her battle is not over. She still recalls her first-ever appearance in an all-male, white-dominated boardroom. As she took her place around the large, highly polished table she couldn't help but second-guess what was on her executive colleagues' minds. They appeared welcoming, but an atmosphere hung in the air. This was... different.

When the first agenda item was raised, Winnie immediately saw the depth of the challenge she faced. 'Please excuse me,' she said, 'but I don't agree...' The room fell silent. She spoke for a minute before picking up on a sense of deep discomfort in the room. No one looked her in the eyes. She assumed she had done something wrong and so kept silent for the remainder of the meeting. Afterwards, she asked the chair what she had done. His answer? 'We invited you to attend but did not expect you to speak.'

Winnie's experience is like those of so many others who are underrepresented in the business world. I've heard first-hand stories like this countless times from senior women leaders working at household name companies. You may think diversity is merely a woke buzzword, but there is a reason organisations are prioritising diversity and inclusion. Different opinions bring challenge. Opposing views are more likely to identify strengths and weaknesses. Contrasts in perspective bring new ways of seeing issues, increasing both opportunities and governance. A variety of beliefs provides balance. Different cultures bring a depth to decision-making that results in decisions that better stand the test of time.

Not having policies in place to support diversity means you are not playing your best team. Sure, you may have enough players, but if you actively support real diversity, your team will be significantly stronger. It can double or triple the talent pool.

Gender diversity

Research consistently shows that as more women are added to a male-dominated senior leadership team, organisations achieve better results. Specifically (and in no particular order), a gender-balanced team means you will:

- **Increase profitability:** Data from FTSE 100, FTSE 250 and Fortune 500 companies has consistently shown a direct causal relationship between the number of women in C-suite positions and a company's profitability.[68] The more women there are in the leadership, the more profitable companies have proved to be.[69]

- **Drive value creation:** In an effort to overcome stereotypes, women have learned to seek out new ways of growing a business. They can excel at building both scalable sustainable companies, while delivering higher-quality customer service. Research has consistently shown that including more women in executive decision-making results in a greater variety of value creation strategies.[70]

- **Be more open, with less risk:** Women are often perceived as more risk averse, perhaps due to the hyper-visibility that comes with representing a minority (in leadership) group and the professional cost of making a mistake, that is, for women, often disastrously magnified.[71] Their presence at the top of an organisation shifts senior leadership teams to be more open to change and with a balanced approach to risk-taking. As a direct consequence, there is often an accompanying shift to increased knowledge building through R&D and less engagement in risky merger and acquisition behaviour.[72]

- **Improve leadership, resilience and employee engagement:** Women score higher than men on most leadership skills.[73] They are also more emotionally intelligent (especially with regard to empathy) than men.[74] This makes them naturally resilient leaders. The need for emotional intelligence has become more acute in the post-Covid world, particularly when it comes to retaining employees and ensuring the workforce is happy, focused and engaged.

- **The fight for social and economic justice:** Women have more experience of adding value to areas that relate to environmental, social and governance (ESG) issues; diversity, equality and inclusion (DEI); and corporate social responsibility (CSR).[75]

The above areas are consistently among the most prominent concerns for shareholders, investors, customers and regulators. As such, enhancing expertise in these areas will lead to more sustainable organisations with greater longevity. Sounds like a no-brainer for any organisation seeking to make an impact, right? Particularly when considered in light of the goal of hiring and retaining top talent to ensure an organisation is able to transform and compete continuously. Sadly, the reason diversity remains on the agenda is that the message doesn't seem to be getting through.

Within the UK, as of July 2023, there were just twenty-three female chief executives of FTSE top 350 companies.[76] There are no black executives working at leadership level of the UK's top 100 companies, whether in the position of CEO, CFO, or chair.[77] As for any sort of pipeline to the top jobs, well, the news there is not good either. At the FTSE board and committee level, the percentage of black directors and non-executive directors is 1.1% – and this figure is dropping. In 2014, the percentage was a giddy 1.3%.[78]

Globally, the figures are equally depressing. If I told you there was a greater than 95% chance of rain, you'd expect it to rain. On the same premise, we can expect all CEOs to be a man. As of July 2022, there were just twenty-four women running Fortune Global 500 companies (4.8%), six of which were women of colour.[79] Ethnic minority women hold a tiny fraction of management positions.[80] Only 5% of all C-suite positions in the USA are women of colour.[81]

The lack of equality is everywhere. When it comes to investment, startups founded by women get, on average, less than 50% of their male-led counterparts. Even a cursory look at the figures would suggest this is not a clever investment strategy: startups founded and co-founded by women generated $0.78 for every $1 of funding, whereas the male-founded startups generated less than half that, at just $0.31 per $1.[82] Think about that for a minute.

While the figures make gloomy reading, not everyone is this short-sighted. There are plenty of disruptive leaders from around the globe who recognise that diversity gives a positive advantage. They've turned that buzz into something incredibly positive. The buzzing draws our attention; the resulting annoyance generates energy to act – that action delivers results.

Hina Nagarajan, the MD and CEO of Diageo India and member of Diageo's executive committee, says she mobilises and supports her diverse team based on her personal beliefs and experiences.

'I've had a great life, but I have also faced most of the challenges that women generally encounter in their career, especially at the mid-career stage. In addition to the inclusion issues you might expect from male-dominated industries, I've had tremendous work-life balance pressure. I had two very young children, a husband travelling 300 days a year on international assignments and a mother who had massive health issues, to attend to. As a manager trying to support my team, any business travel was challenging and getting to parent-teacher meetings almost impossible.

'I have huge empathy for everyone in my team. I've been through it and I've done it all. When I have a meeting with one of my female executives, and five minutes before the meeting she tells me her son is unwell and she has to run to the doctor, I tell her to just go and take care of him. Flexibility as a boss is so important.'

Hina is also highly focused on giving each member of her team an opportunity to shine.

'Every person on the team wants to build a legacy, something that will help them unleash their potential. If I, as a leader, can create a platform for each one of them to fully contribute, unleashing their passion and potential, then this will result in a win for both my people and the company. I sometimes push them onto some crazy targets, but I know they can succeed. I ask the leadership team: "What do we want to stand for? What do you, as a leadership team, want to deliver for this company? What is the impact you want to leave in your stint here?"'

Hina has seen various successes and big results from setting her diverse team some stretching goals. In one, she challenged her team to turn around a low-growth (not failing) division of the drinks company and fulfil a bold mission of tripling its growth. The team managed it – and more – because they were all inspired to make a difference and leave their mark.

'One of the things that has worked really well with goals like this is setting up "sprint teams", which are like task forces. Here, I take eight to ten people from across functions who aren't members of the executive committee, give them a project and empower them to come back with solutions. This has unleashed some real creativity.

'During the pandemic, craft spirits really took off in India. I gave a sprint team a task to launch a product quickly in this space. They did it from start to finish in ninety days. I think we are going to be really big in the craft area now.

'We are creating the leaders of the future by developing them into decision-makers, empowering them to take risks and having their backs in case something goes wrong.'

Every organisation should be looking at the diversity of their team, but a disruptive leader should be thinking about this more than any other. They are operating in a fast-paced environment where constant innovation is required. The key to staying ahead is to embrace the different perspectives that a diverse workplace brings. Ensuring good representation across a company, including in leadership positions, fosters better relationships with the entire team. People feel a greater kinship with their company if they see people like them represented at the top. It is engaging for employees to see that management is not only accepting of other cultures and backgrounds, but there are clear opportunities for anyone to move up in the organisation. The same goes for how customers see you. When a company makes a point of putting diversity on the agenda, it is a clear signal to the outside world that they value inclusivity and that they are working to serve a range of customers. Doesn't it make business sense to broaden your market this way?

Diversity is not simply about gender or ethnicity. It can also encompass different backgrounds and training. Scientific people think differently from those in HR. Those in finance differ from those in sales. Younger people see the world entirely differently from their seniors and have a different range of skills. Organisations are waking up to the opportunities of tapping into their neuro-diverse community – those who see and experience the world differently from their neurotypical counterparts. The challenge to leadership is to garner these differences in viewpoints, and channel them to realise purpose.

Egocentric leaders shy away from diversity. It's much easier to hire in their own image, or so the thinking seems to go. Surrounding yourself with sycophantic, like-minded, 'yes' people from a similar background is the easiest way to stave off difficult conversations. When we all think the same, we can make decisions quicker. But are they the right decisions? The evidence suggests not.

Take, for example, Sam Bankman-Fried, disgraced founder and CEO of FTX. He had the perfect resume – MIT graduate, white, geeky, fitting the much-loved image of VC firms based on all those other successful white Ivy League graduates. He would play the computer game League of Legends while on investor calls. Yet at the time of writing, FTX's investors have lost some $4bn and 'Prosecutors say Bankman-Fried oversaw one of the largest financial frauds in American history.'[83] Rightly, women might ask why so much money was given to Bankman when others who don't fit the stereotype of a successful entrepreneur get nothing.

Yes, diversity is hard work. The word itself implies a variety of experiences, beliefs, behaviours, priorities, world views, cultures, perspectives, understanding... It will mean constant challenge – but that's the point. Team members will collide and the temperature will increase. As we have seen, provided you are united on purpose, the greater the heat, the better. Manage it well and your fire will burn fiercely.

REFLECTIVE EXERCISE: Are you prioritising diversity?

Ask yourself the following:

- What are your genuine beliefs on the subject of diversity?
- Have you reviewed the evidence for increasing diversity?

- Do you actively seek diverse hires when adding to your team (if yes, do you have evidence to support this)?
- What is the experience of diverse candidates within your company?

The importance of empowerment

Ensuring your organisation is full of high performers is a great start, but if they feel stymied at every turn, they won't stick around. Most leaders will, at some point or another, have thought, 'It would be easier to just do it myself.' But if we can't successfully empower others (literally giving away power), we severely limit our growth and opportunities – not to mention that we are almost certainly headed for burnout.

Google's entire ethos was based on empowering its employees.[84] This meant opening up as many 'channels of expression' as possible, to let ideas percolate up from as many different sources as possible. These channels include:

- Google cafes, designed to encourage interactions in and across teams.

- Encouragement to directly email any of the company leaders with ideas and suggestions.

- An innovation management tool called Google Moderator, which is used during tech talks or company-wide meetings. Individuals are invited to ask questions and others can vote up which ones they'd like answered.

- All-hands weekly meetings where employees can ask questions directly to leadership.

- Google Universal Ticketing Systems (GUTS), a way to file issues about anything. These are then reviewed to find patterns of problems.

- 'FixIts' – twenty-four-hour sessions where the Google team drop everything and focus all their energy on solving a specific problem.

- Internal innovation reviews where executives present ideas from their divisions to top executives.

- Googlegeist, an internal survey which solicits feedback on hundreds of issues. Volunteer teams are then appointed to solve the biggest problems.

Google is not perfect, as a quick Google search will show, but they are trying.

The only reason we hire people is because we either don't want to, or cannot, do everything ourselves. If we hire someone who can do a particular job better than us, we are onto a winner. As Steve Jobs once said, 'It doesn't make sense to hire smart people and then tell them what to do. We hire smart people so they can tell us what to do.'[85]

But this only works if we let them do it. If we don't, we exasperate them, and waste our own energy and time. Many organisations speak glowingly about empowerment, but don't quite get it. They'll give team members responsibilities but fail to give them any authority. They will, for example, set up a working group to resolve a complex organisational issue, but then put in place a structure where no decisions can be made without the full authorisation of the leaders to whom the working group reports. Or individuals will work on a deal in the belief that they have the go-ahead to see it to fruition, only to be pulled up at the eleventh hour because the outcome seems too risky or not quite to the manager's liking.

Empowerment is only effective when a leader gives over some genuine power, authority and resources to another individual in order to get a job done. Therein lies the real power to grow your business. This is a key challenge every leader has to rise to: leading those who have skills and expertise we will never have. Often, the kind of leadership we need is 'servant leadership'. Instead of telling, we must *ask*. 'How can I help you do your job better? What do you need from me?' If you are serious about increasing your fuel, you need to be very good at true empowerment.

REFLECTIVE EXERCISE: Being an empowering leader

Increase your levels of delegation and empowerment by asking each of your direct reports the following:

- What am I involved in that a leader at my level shouldn't be?

- What am I not involved in that a leader at my level should be?

- When I delegate to you, do I give you the power/
  resources you need to do the job?

None of this is to say you need to hand everything over and let people get on with it. As we saw from the Google example above, it takes a team effort. Information is passed up and down the firm and freely shared. No one works in a vacuum. 'Collective identity' is the type of leadership that is rated highest by followers and one that encourages everyone to feel a sense of shared purpose.[86] Such leaders internalise company values, consistently act in ways that benefit group interests, use 'we' and 'us' language and engage in fewer self-serving behaviours. This is the polar opposite of leaders who are motivated by narcissistic tendencies, who seem hell-bent on asserting their authority at every turn. These leaders, who think and act as though they are superior in every way, are, perhaps not surprisingly, seen as the most ineffective.

There are plenty of examples throughout corporate history where organisations have relentlessly pursued an individualistic leadership identity. This usually goes hand in hand with abusive behaviours and often ends spectacularly badly. We talked earlier about Enron's famous 'rank and yank' culture, but Lay and Shilling were not the only leaders to act in this way. Fred Goodwin, the former chief executive of Royal Bank of Scotland (RBS), earned the nickname 'Fred the Shred' thanks to his habit of regularly 'shredding' people in front of colleagues if they earned his displeasure.[87] The practice of continually yelling and bawling at a team clearly had an impact: RBS was one of the first casualties of the 2008/9 financial crisis and had to be rescued with a £45 billion bailout, coming within hours of running out of cash completely. One of the reasons cited for its collapse was the bank's vulnerability, thanks to the sheer weight of a series of misguided takeovers that Fred the Shred had bulldozed through. Would it have been different if any of the senior executives had been allowed to have a voice and block such clearly risky moves? We'll never know. What we do know, as we discussed previously, is that negative behavioural dispositions can be constrained through ensuring effective accountability to strong behavioural norms, incentives for specific types of (good) behaviours and clear expectations concerning what behaviours will be rewarded and punished.

Ego-driven leaders do not like constraints. Who does? Yet the best-run companies (and those that are more likely to pass the test of time) are run by leaders who make themselves truly accountable. They are available to their board, their employees, their investors and their customers. Governance is a big deal in these companies, and for good reason. It is worth highlighting, after the previous section on diversity, that of the eighteen-strong members of the RBS board during the Fred the Shred era, all but one (a white woman) were white males.[88] Diverse boards are needed to bring in diversity of thought, challenge and proper oversight.

Effective leadership encourages constructive dissent, rather than destructive consent. Again, contrast this with Fred Goodwin's leadership tactics of brutally quizzing his RBS managers at 9.30am each day, openly questioning their worth – hardly an atmosphere conducive to encouraging innovative thought.

REFLECTIVE EXERCISE: Accountability

Ask yourself the following questions:

- Would you want to work for you? If so, why?
- Who are you accountable to?
- Who have you given tacit permission to speak openly in order to challenge your thinking without recrimination?
- Imagine tomorrow's leading news item is the decision or behaviour you are desperately keeping a secret. What would you do differently?
- What is the advantage of you being accountable?

Succession planning

Once a fire has been lit and is burning well, the challenge becomes keeping it alight over the long term. If the organisation is built around a particularly strong leader, succession becomes more of a challenge. Truly great leaders recognise that the purpose they're trying to achieve is much bigger than their own success. As such, they actively plan for others to take the reins.

Sir Alex Ferguson, manager of Manchester United Football Club (MUFC), left the club in 2013 after twenty-six highly successful years. After he left, MUFC churned through eight managers in less than ten years (David Moyes, Ryan Giggs, Louis van Gaal, Jose Mourinho and Ole Gunnar Solskjaer, Michael Carrick (caretaker), Ralf Rangnick (interim) and Erik ten Hag). There had been no succession plan. Compare this to rival club Liverpool FC. When the great Bill Shankly OBE retired in 1974, the club's famous Boot Room[89] supplied the next four managers (Bob Paisley, Joe Fagan, Kenny Dalglish and Roy Evans) over the subsequent twenty years. True succession planning doesn't happen by accident. It is deliberate and requires energy and time.

If you are running an enterprise with no clearly defined succession plan understood by the board, then you have planned for your organisation to fail. The same is true for whatever function or division you lead within your business. It is worse than dying without a will. Every ounce of energy you have spent, risks coming to naught. Some legacy.

To return once more to the theme of diversity (because it can't be over-emphasised), leaders need to recruit successors from a wider pool. One of the biggest hurdles to overcome here is unconscious bias. When it comes to those top jobs, we tend to gravitate towards people who look and sound like us. Imagine a highly successful CFO called John who works for a global engineering firm. John attended the top school and university in the country, is white and fifty-five years old when he signals his intent to leave. For the CEO, it would be natural to think about recruiting someone just like John – and why not? He was a great success, the executives knew and respected how he worked, investors liked him – ergo, let's find another John. It seems the safe option. But is it the right option? It sounds rather like sticking with the status quo to me – Level One thinking. As already stated, there are many proven benefits to diversity at every level in a business and that includes your job.

I've worked with some incredible executives across the world and have seen first-hand the difference diversity can make at the top of organisations. I love interviewing, coaching and hearing from top Indian CEOs (for example) because they have such a different life experience, cultural background and perspective on the world than those I work with in the West. I come out of those meetings hoping for more Indian CEOs in Fortune and FTSE companies, as they are typically much more attuned to spirituality, community and ensuring a positive societal change. They see the world differently, so they think differently – and that is a good thing. They have a different energy. They seem to have more time (though clearly that is impossible) and they prioritise people.

It is a bold move for a company to make a perhaps unexpectedly diverse hire (as CEO, or onto a board, or wider leadership team), but get it right, and they reap the benefits of innovation and a change of perspective. During onboarding, ensure that they are set up for success with the right support. The pressure on a diverse candidate is higher as they represent the minority, rather than the majority. The organisation that encourages people to ask difficult questions, and gives everyone time to figure out the answers, is the one that thrives. This is truly disruptive leadership.

REFLECTIVE EXERCISE: Succession planning

Is your succession planning bold and diverse, or does it repeat the formula of the past? Who will be your successor? Do they look/sound like you?

8
Increasing Oxygen

As one of *Forbes'* 'Most Powerful Women' and ranked among the top ten 'Best Chief Marketing Officers' in Brazil, Daniela Cachich, co-president at Ambev / AB InBev, knows a thing or two about how to gain much-needed oxygen for a fire without throwing caution to the wind.

> 'I want to challenge everything. I want to change everything. But we have to proceed with caution and wisdom. We need to be incredibly astute in our actions and display unwavering resilience, as the system is designed to discourage disruption.'

When Daniela first joined a challenger company in Brazil as the chief marketing officer, her budget was a mere 1% of what the largest player in the market was spending. What's more, her previous CEO had warned that accepting the role was a colossal mistake. If that wasn't enough, she faced the challenge of joining a strongly masculine culture where, as a woman, she was expected to fail. She told me how:

> 'As a disruptor, I didn't want to adopt
> the traditional "masculinist" approach
> to marketing.'

While she put an end to adverts objectifying women, she didn't want to be seen solely as a woman fighting against this practice.

> 'We want to disrupt, but we don't want
> to explicitly state it. It's important to use
> language that makes others feel secure. I knew
> that if I wasn't careful, people would label me
> as a crazy woman.'

Despite the challenges, Daniela achieved remarkable success, growing the company's market share from 0% to 20% in just five years. This wasn't an isolated triumph. With CMO stints at Unilever, PepsiCo and now Ambev / AB InBev, her achievements demonstrate her expertise in gaining market share and revitalising global brands. She explained:

> 'When you're seeking to invigorate your
> brand, you must remember that consumers

don't want to simply relate to products; they crave the stories that these brands tell.'

Daniela always strives to connect people and communities – the all-important oxygen – with a brand's purpose through storytelling.

'When people approach me with a new innovation, often emphasising functionality and ticking off a checklist, I always ask, "What else can we do? What impact can we make?" Every leader should pose this question. The answer may involve casting a minority group in adverts or donating a portion of profits to charity. We take the volume of sales for granted; I want to know what additional value we can provide.'

For startups with great products that are struggling to gain traction (oxygen), Daniela is quick to point out that purpose alone is not enough. A focus on procurement, finance, governance and distribution is also critical to success.

'I've been successful in challenging the status quo because I had robust distribution networks. You want people to repeatedly buy your product, so quality and availability are crucial. The fundamentals must be in place, as competition is fierce, and gaining market share is costly. This helps explain

why large corporations thrive – they have the
fundamentals at scale.'

By necessity, startups tend to be infatuated with their
products. But Daniela stressed the importance of
being able to answer the question of why someone
else would choose to purchase them.

'If your product is merely a "nice to have",
people are less likely to become repeat
customers. Even within larger corporates,
purpose and fundamentals should be
balanced 50/50; otherwise, profitability will
suffer. That's why I tailor my messaging
to stakeholders.'

When faced with larger competitors seeking to steal
market share, Daniela cautioned against attempting to
match them financially. Understanding their strengths
and weaknesses is crucial and finding ways to capture market share in an essential yet weaker niche area
can be much more effective. Their arrogance may lead
them to underestimate you as a competitor until it's
too late.

Disruption is far from easy, Daniela counselled.

'Find a way to muster your courage each day.
The system is designed to prove that change
is a bad idea, that challenging the status quo
is ill-advised. Why do I persist? It's not for
ego; it's for the transformation I'm driving.

Disruptive leaders aren't in it for their careers; they believe in something greater. They take significant risks, with a higher likelihood of being fired than promoted.

'I believe in something that maybe the company doesn't. It requires tremendous resilience over the medium to long term. That's why I surround myself with individuals who want to lead and disrupt alongside me. I seek people who share my passion for disruption. Many individuals approach it from the angle of something that's "crazy" or "impossible". Be comfortable being the first to take action; the first to raise the necessity of challenging the status quo. You must embrace discomfort. Disruptive leaders aspire to look back and say, "That was my legacy."'

The winds of change

Success can come quickly if you take advantage of the prevailing conditions. The seller of water bottles on a hot day outside a music festival will do brisk business. Ditto the street stall full of umbrellas during a sudden and unexpected downpour. These entrepreneurs have spotted an opportunity and have taken full advantage of it. Such successes, though, tend to be short-lived – a flash in the pan. Standing the test of time, over decades or even centuries, is very, very difficult.

It entails exploiting the prevailing conditions, as well as any lucky breaks, and turning this into a solid long-term proposition, all the while dealing with potential threats that try to starve your venture of oxygen.

I coached two entrepreneurs who, after deciding to step out of the rat race, did some research, took some courses and set up an Amazon shop. They chose to focus on a specific eye serum (one of them was a beautician) and invested in product design and labels. They bought 1,000 bottles of the serum for £5 each and sold them all at £95 each. It was a fantastic return. They ordered more and sold more. Soon, they were on track to earn £3 million. They had a product the market wanted and a limitless supply. It was akin to bringing a match to petrol. Imagine their excitement.

But it wasn't long before competitors took note of their success. Established beauty brands produced rival products, promoting them heavily as they entered the market. Aggressive price reductions followed. Just to up the ante, the competitors penned a few negative reviews on my entrepreneurs' pages. The price war quickly took its toll. Cutbacks needed to be made and, meanwhile, their competitors spent heavily on promoting their alternative products. Within a short space of time, the original serum firm was too starved of cash to compete. Three years after launch, they closed.

There is nothing so exciting as having the right product, in the right place, at the right time. It breeds an incredible sense of invincibility. Like paragliding, it is exhilarating, exciting and endorphin-releasing. It might kill you, but oh what fun. Those of you who have experienced it will know what I mean. It will be one of the best periods of your working life. The key is to sustain that momentum. You need your customers to come back, week after week, year after year. They are the oxygen your fire needs to keep burning.

Successful disruptors find different ways to maintain momentum. Samsung, the home appliance and mobile technology conglomerate, works on multiple new product projects simultaneously, in the hope that one of them will be what the customer wants. Its digital rival Apple does the opposite, generally focusing on just one major project and then trying to convince (or change) the market to buy it once it's released. Amazon innovates across a range of markets to keep its offering fresh, from cashier-free stores to AI-powered home robots, to an online healthcare service. There are multiple routes to success.

The prevailing conditions can be a gift, but if a disruptive leader does not exploit them and continue to do so, they can also be a threat. Something will change and what once seemed easy will suddenly become hard. The winds shift. Oxygen is depleted. Fire starts to burn out. If you don't shift with the conditions – or, better still, stay ahead – a smoky smouldering mess will follow, until all that is left is charred remains. This is exactly what happened to Nokia.

Most people reading this book have probably owned a Nokia phone at some point. By the year 2000, Nokia was the largest company in Europe.[90] At its pinnacle in 2007, the Helsinki-based firm had 49.4% of the global market share in mobile phones,[91] contributing

25% of Finland's GDP and a market capital value of $110 billion. To put this into context, in 2021 Apple had a roughly 28% market share. Its success was, as the Finnish Finance Minister of the time stated, 'an economic miracle.'[92]

But the prevailing conditions changed and Nokia failed to take heed. Its thinking was still based firmly in 1992, when Jorma Ollila took over as CEO and redefined the company's purpose in a bid to compete with the then-growing competitor, Motorola, as well as a number of Japanese telecoms rivals. The new purpose was 'life goes mobile', with a stated priority of reducing phone size (early mobiles were the size of bricks) and improving battery life, so that Nokia phones would become a highly portable, must-have gadget. To begin with, the strategy was a huge success – hence the 49.4% market share. Nokia stuck doggedly to its goal of reducing phone size and increasing battery life. Unfortunately, the wind that had made them so successful was changing direction. Competitors' products entered the market, and customers' demands changed. 'Life goes mobile' now meant different things. When Apple introduced its app-based iPhone in 2007, it was streets ahead of Nokia's Symbian device-based phones. One year later, when Android launched (the Google operating system used on almost all non-Apple phones today), Nokia was reluctant to adopt the system, ignoring the example set by Samsung, Motorola and Huawei. It was a further year before the Finnish phone company began to react, bringing in new, outside leadership from Microsoft, but it was already too late. By 2012, just five years after the iPhone first appeared, Nokia was showing losses into the billions. Its mobile phone division was sold off to Microsoft in what turned out to be a disastrous deal for the buyer, which later wrote off $7.6bn on the Nokia acquisition.[93]

Early warnings were discernible from the early 2000s, when smartphones began to emerge. Yet, Nokia believed rigidly in its king-of-the-cellphone status, producing durable, affordable, traditional cellphones, just when customers were eyeing the exciting, sleek smartphones and all the apps that came with them. By the time they began to react, it was too late. There was no oxygen left. The fires lit by Nokia's competitors had stolen it all.

When to adjust oxygen levels

As any firefighter will tell you, reduce the flow of oxygen and your fire shrinks. The opposite is also true: increase the flow of oxygen and the fire will grow in intensity. This is why firefighters spend a lot of time studying wind direction. The moment the wind changes, they know that they must immediately refocus their efforts in the new direction. Firefighters die because of rapidly changing conditions. If they underestimate the speed of the fire fuelled by changing winds, they could quickly get surrounded and caught out. It is no different in business. Often, though, the change in wind direction can be less obvious.

While leaders talk a lot about potential threats and challenges, talking about them and fully understanding where they come from are two different things. Most of us, perhaps understandably, tend to focus on variables we are familiar with. This makes us vulnerable to disruptive threats that seem to come from nowhere. How much, for example, did the global pandemic take you by surprise? Was it something your organisation was able to adapt to quickly? Or did it take months to restabilise?

Amy Webb, the founder of the Future Today Institute, has identified eleven sources of potential change and disruption that can affect organisations.[94] They are:

- Wealth distribution

- Education

- Infrastructure

- Government

- Geopolitics

- Economics

- Public health

- Demographics

- Environment

- Media and telecommunications

- Technology

How much would a sudden shift in any of these areas impact your business? Each has the capacity to do so. Potential external threats to your business are so much greater than simply a new competitor entering your market, or an existing rival taking a big leap forward with a new 'must-have' product. There could be a change in the legislative landscape that might restrict your business model; the wider economy may be spooked by a sudden market collapse; a war might break out causing global ramifications (such as Russia's invasion of Ukraine); the beginning of a bull market could change the trading landscape, putting pressure on your manufacturing process; an entirely new technology may emerge; an investor might challenge your strategy, or instigate a hostile takeover.

In all cases, it helps to be prepared for the unexpected. When the Covid-19 pandemic hit, US telecom giant Verizon, which had more than 1,600 corporate stores and 30,000 employees servicing its 110 million customers, faced some tough decisions. With customers staying away from stores, either to avoid contact with others or because of mandatory lockdowns, this looked like a challenge by any measure. But it was also an opportunity, says Verizon's Consumer Group COO Krista Bourne:

> 'This is where five-year strategies matter. We already had that in place, so we had our North Star and knew where we wanted to be. Before we even got to this moment, we understood

what made sense for the business from a customer standpoint. We knew how they were engaging with channels and it allowed us to leverage some of the digital investments we'd already been making with things like in-store pick-up and appointments. We had the opportunity to bring this all together and reassure our teams, customers and business partners that this was our strategy, we were not off course. Then, we needed to thread the needle between what we needed to do on a temporary basis, and what would work well permanently. We were very clear with everyone about what would be temporary or permanent, since things that are temporary are harder for people to adopt.'

While some businesses chose to permanently shutter stores in favour of adopting a digital model, Verizon has decided to keep most of them open following the worst of the pandemic. In its updated five-year plan, it was agreed that, despite the fixed cost, the stores played a role over and above that of a single sale. Customers rely on the outlets for face-to-face consultations with Verizon experts, for troubleshooting and to get broken phones fixed. Krista and her team also used the opportunity to reflect on other aspects of the business model.

'Early on in the pandemic, we redeployed 10,000 previously store-based employees into other roles, primarily customer service. This got us thinking: was this the future? A hybrid employee that can do sales and service? It opened our eyes to what might be possible. I don't think we'd have seen it that way without that moment. We were careful to pay attention because it pushed our thinking.'

If you are ready for risks and prepared to react, there are always opportunities. Ask yourself: What are the risks facing me right now? Are there any potential threats looming?

At any moment, an organisation stuck in the status quo can be disrupted, seemingly without warning. As an example, in November 2022 an artificial intelligence product hit the market. OpenAI's ChatGPT tool became available on the internet. With it, users were able to write simple or complex prompts – with frankly astonishing results. The tool is able to write self-documenting software code with comments; letters that have been successful in appealing against parking or speeding fines; legal contracts; responses to customer complaints (using different personalities and tones of voices, – including your own); a business plan to enter a new market; and much, much more. So much more, in fact, that in March 2023 high-profile technology leaders (including Elon Musk) wrote an open letter basically begging AI companies to pause the training of new super-powerful systems for six months, saying that recent advances in AI presented 'profound risks to society and humanity.'[95]

Disruption comes from all angles, is often unexpected and can risk everything you do today. If risk management is not on your agenda, start with Porter's Five Forces model,[96] and a SWOT or PESTEL analysis. But being open to diverse (there's that word again) input and perspective is key. Success requires an ability to read the direction of the wind to minimise any threat to your company.

REFLECTIVE EXERCISE: Risk management

Ask yourself the following questions:

- What threat are you ignoring that could destroy all you have built?
- What external perspective are you gaining to ensure you are abreast of the threats facing your industry?

Reaction to disruptive threats

What, then, are our options when dealing with disruptive threats? Most organisations, when threatened, tend to react in one of three ways: freeze, fight or flight. Let's look at each of these possible responses.

Freeze

When facing adversity, some leaders might freeze. They become passive, disengaged and ineffective. They may even convince themselves that what is going on is not actually a threat after all. It feels safer to bury their head in the sand. 'It may go away.' So they ignore the data. Or decide the team that raised the issue is wrong. Or the customers who have been making complaints are just whining. Or the suppliers say it can't be done. Or the markets don't understand an entrepreneurial business. People don't know what they are talking about.

Paralysis and lack of action impact all departments or organisations in the same way. In the face of falling revenues as a result of the threat, or an increase in poor reviews, or however the threat begins to manifest itself, employees will become fearful. Emulating the reaction of the leader, they will freeze too. Deadlines will be missed. Customer service slides. Sales slow. The threat becomes a self-fulfilling prophecy thanks to a woeful lack of action. The Nokia story illustrates the compound effect of failing to acknowledge a threat. It is not an isolated example. There are plenty of instances of once-dominant organisations that dismissed a threat and paid the price. Take Blockbuster – founded in 1985, it once had over 9,000 video rental stores worldwide, with 84,300 staff. At one point, Blockbuster were opening a new store every seventeen hours. As of 2022, just one franchise store was still operating, in Oregon, USA. The threat? Digital music and film downloads. Blockbuster froze in the face of the obvious threat. Even when the company had the opportunity to buy Netflix in 2000, its executives still felt they knew better.[97]

Another example is Woolworths Group,[98] founded in the UK in 1909 and affectionately known as 'Woolies'. At one time, it had 800 high street stores, with 27,000 staff.[99] During the nineties, it was the number one retailer of music and famous for its pick and mix sweets. But in 2009, all its high street stores were shut down, although its website limped along until 2015. Like Blockbuster, Woolworths froze in the face of competition. Two key disruptive forces were not taken into account: the shift to digital, and the move away from the high street to out-of-town retail parks.

What are you avoiding right now? What do you need to do? What is stopping you?

Fight

The term 'fighting fire with fire' has been attributed to Shakespeare who, in *King John* (1595), wrote:

'Be stirring as the time, be fire with fire.
Threaten the threatener and outface the brow
Of bragging horror ...'

These three lines are highly emotive, suggesting that, when threatened, we turn to more extreme methods than we would usually. We match aggression with aggression, violence with violence.

Many leaders relish the opportunity to meet a challenge head-on. They stand up to a threat and trade blows, however formidable the opponent. A threatened terrier doesn't care about the odds when fighting a bigger dog. They might lose, but they will die trying.

Are you facing a threat right now and trying to figure out whether you have the stomach to fight it? It is worthwhile asking yourself this question, for the cost can be great.

Where are you fighting right now? Is it worth the fight? Will winning the fight help you achieve your primary objective?

Flight

Flight is where we figure out an escape plan and use it. We run away. All that is seen is the soles of our feet and dust.

Sometimes flight is the best option. In 2006, Liverpool FC were playing West Ham in the FA Cup Final, and I went with two friends by train to see the match. A fight broke out in the carriage a few metres away. I'd never been in this situation before and was fascinated. Being more streetwise, my friends grabbed me and forcefully moved me away from the trouble. Flight can often be wise.

But there are other times when fleeing is cowardice. Think here of the business owner who deliberately drains the company of cash before declaring it bankrupt. The director who commits fraud and flees to another country. A manager who disappears in the heat of battle, leaving decisions to others. When things go wrong, we respect those who hold their hands up and say: 'I'm sorry, it was my fault. I got it wrong.'

What are you running away from? Is it wise? Or is it cowardly?

Dealing with wildfires

Every so often, your business will be hit by a wildfire; a fire that feels completely out of control and threatens to destroy everything in its path, including you. These events are typically rare yet many companies faced this exact scenario during the global Covid-19 pandemic (and then with the Russian invasion that created supply chain issues, higher energy costs and other challenges). How you deal with them is central to surviving the challenge and moving on to flourish in the aftermath. The story of another phone company, the South Korean firm Samsung, is a good illustration of how this is possible. This time, there is a happy ending.

Samsung launched its much-anticipated Galaxy S7 mobile phone range in August 2016, beating rival Apple's iPhone 7 launch. It was, the press hype said, the best Android phone of its generation. The Samsung S7 range included the concept of the 'phablet', or big phone, one that was slightly larger than a smartphone (but smaller than a tablet) and packed full of high-tech features including an improved camera, better screen definition and a longer battery life.

Just five days after the launch, things began to unravel. A news report appeared, talking about a Galaxy Note S7 'exploding'.[100] Pictures began to appear online of the burned, charred remains of various S7 models.[101] In the days that followed, a PR nightmare ensued as social media filled with discussions about this worrying development. Compounding the disaster, many airlines banned the phones from flights. During every pre-flight briefing, Samsung's S7 was named and shamed. 'If you have a Samsung S7, we'd ask you to alert the flight team. It needs to be removed from the flight because of the fire risk...' Can you imagine how damaging this was?

You don't need to imagine. Samsung's Q3 profits plunged 30% after the company announced a global recall of 2.5 million Galaxy S7 phones, blaming faulty batteries. The loss of confidence in the brand was estimated to have cost the business $5.3bn. In Q4, Samsung lost its spot as the world's top mobile phone company to its old rival, Apple.[102] Just when things looked like they couldn't get worse, the replacement handsets that were issued to customers following the mass recall (with assurances that they were safe to use) also started to catch fire. In one incident, an entire Southwest Airlines flight in the US had to be evacuated after a phone on board began emitting smoke.

The problem with the replacement phones led to serious questions being asked about Samsung's crisis management abilities and product safety testing. With major US carriers such as AT&T and T-Mobile declaring that they were no longer issuing the S7 replacements, Samsung announced that anyone in possession of one of the phones needed to power it down and stop using it. The entire S7 range was withdrawn from sale entirely.

This was, by any measure, a wildfire. The only way to stop a wildfire is to remove heat, fuel or oxygen (or more than one of these). What Samsung did next is an object lesson in stopping and then recovering from the devastating aftermath of a wildfire.

First, the firm owned up to the faults, communicated clearly and ceased all sales of the S7. Second, Samsung issued a recall of those phones already sold. Its disaster-recovery processes kicked in and they sent three boxes to each customer: an antistatic bag, insulation layers and gloves for handling their phone. By removing all phones from the market and from customers, they removed the fuel (the faulty phones) and cut off the oxygen source (bad publicity).

Samsung also took note that product recalls are notoriously difficult to enforce, typically generating a low return rate, and executed a proactive strategy. Staff were sent to major airports to exchange handsets/refund customers who possessed the S7, and Samsung asked network carriers to update the phone software so that the S7s could no longer be electrically recharged. This strategy resulted in customers returning 96% of all phones sold. It was a phenomenal result. The total estimated cost to Samsung of implementing these steps was $3.1bn.

The final move was to build a new test lab staffed with 700 researchers, 200,000 devices and 30,000 batteries. Once Samsung had found the cause of the issue, they were transparent and honest in their communication. The blame was attributed to battery casing that was too small and an abnormal weld spot. They created a Battery Advisory Group, which included experts from around the world, and designed an eight-point battery safety system standard that other smartphone vendors would be free to use. Perhaps understandably, the launch of the S8 and S8 Note in 2017 was going to be a challenge. The new smartphone had to be exceptional to attract customers back. Most importantly, they needed not to catch fire. The S8 Note was packed full of tech that meant – remarkably, considering Samsung's recent history – it was quickly established as the market-leading Android phone. It was safe, too. The astonishingly quick recovery from the wildfire was confirmed when, in April 2017, a ReportLinker survey found that 89% of Samsung's customers would buy a phone from them again, and 66% of non-Samsung customers would consider buying one.[103] Perhaps most importantly in regard to its prospects for the future, Samsung regained the top slot in the league of mobile phones. Their oxygen was flowing again.

As Samsung showed, a wildfire, even a high-profile one, doesn't need to take a business down. But a quick response is vital to stop it from burning out of control. This requires being honest about the issue, communicating well and sharing the results widely to build trust among all stakeholders.

Sometimes, it is possible to anticipate wildfires and, if not entirely see off any of the potential dangers, at least take steps to ensure it doesn't get out of control. Indeed, it is possible to work with the fire, if it burns hotter or longer than expected. I've already mentioned artificial intelligence, or AI as it is more commonly known. While the idea of AI has been around since the 1950s, it is only recently that the true extent of its capabilities has started to be explored. You don't have to watch dystopian movies like *Terminator* to realise that there are real fears that machines could get out of control and even take over. This is something very much on the mind of IBM's Chief Privacy and Trust Officer, Christina Montgomery, who told me:

> 'AI has so much potential to solve so many societal problems and to make a difference in the world, if it's used the right way. We're the oldest company in tech and have been deploying new technology responsibly for over 100 years, so there is a real opportunity. However, while we need to share an optimistic perspective, we also understand the downside risks of what can happen when AI is done wrong. We want to help to address this early on with a set of common beliefs and principles.'

Christina comes from a legal background and views herself as a 'lawyer growing up in a technology company'. Her view is that a risk-based approach needs to be adopted in order to build trust in AI.

> 'There are legal basics in, say, intellectual property law that every lawyer has to understand. It's the same with anti-trust,

or competition law, contracts or contractual rights. But there is nothing about AI and, as yet, no call for it either. When IBM started to create governance around AI, it was not that we had to. We did it because we wanted to build trust and we believe the best way to do that is to show we are putting the guardrails in.

'You're always going to have bad actors. We've been very clear about our own values and principles around what we will do and what we won't do. We don't, for example, offer general purpose facial recognition technology, because we can't be sure, even if it's 100% accurate with every individual around the world, that it's being used responsibly in different sectors. We hold a lot of discussions, inside and outside the company, because we want to ensure that we're getting as many people on board as possible to contribute to our point of view and perspective. It's really important that the standards that eventually get adopted in this space are dictated by those with the same values and principles as IBM. That's to all of our benefit.'

REFLECTIVE EXERCISE: How will you tackle a wildfire?

Work your way through the following steps:

1. Take one specific new technology (such as AI) and list every way it could positively or negatively impact your business. Then ask a twenty-one-year-old computer science graduate (or similar) to do the same. Finally, pay a researcher to repeat the task and review all competitive threats facing your company.

2. Think about how much time and energy you're putting into checking the 'weather forecast' – in other words, looking for any changing headwinds you can take advantage of, or that will cause an existential crisis.

3. Do you have a plan based on real evidence (rather than a whim) that will allow you not just to survive but gain from a change in circumstances following a wildfire?

PART FOUR
TROUBLESHOOTING

9

When Your Fire Dies Or Is Out Of Control: Dealing With Failure

It was 2007 and my technology consulting company had just had a year of record revenues. Turnover had increased by over 50% and profits by 300%. The business couldn't recruit fast enough and skirted on the edge of overtrading, where we might not be able to deliver the work we'd committed to, due to a lack of staff and cash. We'd won a number of multi-year deals worth millions of pounds, which had opened doors into very large organisations.

Our track record within financial services was growing. Swiss Re, now sited within the famous 'Gherkin' London landmark, had been a key customer for over five years. My regular meetings with the SVP of Infrastructure Services in the capital's swankiest restaurants were a joy. HBOS flew their staff from around the UK to our training suite in the Midlands.

Then there was Standard & Poor's, CMC Group PLC (for whom we provided five-minute response times, twenty-four hours a day, seven days a week), Lloyds Bank, the Pension Insurance Corporation, KPMG and others.

It seemed we could do no wrong. All we needed to do to continue our meteoric growth was keep investing in our people and systems. Meanwhile, I was trying my hardest to strengthen my senior management team to help drive the business forward. All the signs were good when a competitor of a similar size sold out at circa fourteen times EBITDA and the owners walked away as multimillionaires. It confirmed to me that this was a prime time to be in the Oracle marketplace, a conviction further fuelled by multiple buy-out offers. I turned every one down, convinced we would continue to grow and soon be in an even better place. I doubled down on my strategy, reinvesting 75% of our profits into a financial services division. The investment included provision for a team of very expensive delivery and sales staff, with all the systems and infrastructure that came with that, but we had a tailwind now. These were heady times.

Feeling more confident by the day, we pitched for and successfully won significant contracts with blue-chip firms such as UBS and JP Morgan. Again, I was convinced that this was only the start of something even bigger. The contracts were, after all, just phase one of multi-year, high-value deals. Winning them had provided the catalyst for the step change in business size we were heading for. The big banks told us to expect the orders to be rubber-stamped within a week's time. It was a formality. We'd won the deal, jumped through the procurement hoops and were now waiting for the board to sign off on the contract.

The end of the week came and went. 'Sorry,' we were told when we tentatively chased. 'We don't know why it was delayed, but don't worry, it will be signed off at next month's board meeting.' An agonising month later, we received terrible news from both would-be clients: 'Sorry, all projects have been put on hold.'

Days later, Lehman Brothers was no more and the whole banking industry was in turmoil. The US government bailed out AIG. In the UK and across Europe there were queues outside banks, and more major bailouts followed. We were in the midst of the 2008/9 global crash that pulled the rug on many established major banks. It also swept away the oxygen required for investment, growth and profitability.

In 2011, I sold the business for 15% of what it had been worth before the financial crisis. There are no words to describe the crushing sense of failure I felt.

Why do we fail?

Every leader wants to be successful. As such, many seek to identify and apply the formula others have used in a bid to duplicate their success. But there is a problem with this approach.

David McRaney has spent considerable time researching just how common success is. It turns out, it's pretty rare. His research led him to the experiences of US Navy chiefs during World War Two.[104] They'd set out to increase pilot survival rates from the circa 50% for any given bombing raid. They reviewed every returning plane and decided to strengthen those areas where most bullets had struck.

The Navy bosses turned to a brilliant statistician, Abraham Wald,[105] to find out what he thought of their plan and were taken aback when he vehemently disagreed with their proposals. Wald noted that the study had only considered the *surviving* aircraft. The bombers that had been shot down were, of course, not available for analysis. He argued that the holes in the returning aircraft represented areas where a bomber *could* take damage and still return home safely. Rather than shoring up those areas that had done their job, the Navy should focus its efforts on reinforcing the areas where the returning aircraft were unscathed, as all signs indicated that these were areas that, if hit, would cause the plane to be lost.

In our pursuit of success, we often do the same as the US Navy chiefs did. We give too much attention to the survivors without taking into consideration *why* they survived and others failed. In so doing, we introduce and reinforce three recurring problems:

1. Funding

2. Bias

3. Ignoring lessons

Funding

History appears to tell us that successful companies in the USA/Europe are those led by white, well-educated, middle-class men. Given a choice, most investors wouldn't think of backing anyone different. Just ask female and/or BAME founders. Data shows that 68% of funding goes to startups founded by all-male teams; 29% goes to mixed-gender teams and just 3% to all-female teams.[106] What's more, startups with a female founder get less money, even when they are more successful. There is a reason that investors threw money at Sam Bankman-Fried, the failed CEO of FTX, whereas black female founders get less than 1% of the total funding available.

Bias

Organisations tend to recruit with the same bias that causes inequalities in investment, creating an endless circle of bias in the process. This is why most organisations, from the shop floor to board level, look broadly the same. When it comes to promoting anyone from within, they are all fishing from a similar-looking pool. I spoke to the HR director of a major national business newspaper in the UK who was trying to fix this issue but didn't know how to. He told me:

> 'We are full of male Oxbridge types, which means we have no diversity. When we hire different, they don't stick around because of the presiding culture.'

219

As detailed earlier, a lack of diversity means we miss out on innovation, governance and purposeful disruption.

Ignoring lessons

In our haste to recover, move on and put mistakes behind us, we miss the important lessons to be learned from failures. When was the last time you read a book by someone who tried and failed? Doing so might redefine the concept for you. It may also help you to strengthen your weak areas, just like those Navy chiefs.

In the case of my technology consultancy, I took a long, hard look at where I went wrong and learned some invaluable lessons. I can see that I should have taken the time to gain external energy and input before the financial crash. It would have helped me to be more aware of what was going on around me. I should have read relevant articles and taken advice from the right people, which would have helped me invest in a different way. I should have focused more on Level Two and Three thinking/learning, asking the difficult questions and inviting questions from elsewhere. At the time, I was convinced that I was open to ideas, a real team player. I prided myself on it. Paradoxically, I also felt that I was different and knew better. But I didn't, and like almost everyone else, I paid the price.

Perhaps I am being hard on myself. Being a team player is not always easy. According to Munera Al Dosari, CEO of leading technology and retailer

Starlink, it takes time, and sometimes a leap of faith, to trust everyone around you. Starlink is part of the Ooredoo Group of companies, which began life in 2006 as a retailer for mobiles and mobile accessories. As well as becoming the fastest-growing retailer in Qatar, it is now also one of the largest outsource-managed services providers in multiple fields including IT, installations, maintenance and contract centres. Exploration and discovery are at the heart of the company philosophy, which means there is a lot of pressure on the team to keep up with changes in the industry and shape the future of the company. She told me:

'For me, this business is all about agility. To grow the company, I need to choose the right people in order to expand, as well as have the finances to support the vision.

'Easily the hardest part of my journey as a leader is gaining the trust of my team. When you have the right team, and they support you, anything is possible. I also need to take into account that there is a risk with hiring, too. This is a fast-growing company. I'm putting them on my balance sheet and I might not get a return on my investment. Sometimes this gives me a big warning light, but as an entrepreneur, you need to take that risk.

'The way I balance all of this is to build our human relationships and spend time sharing.

It's not about segregating my business life
and personal life, but about finding a mutual
ground between both sides. I consider these
guys friends, and we actually enjoy our time
together going out for lunch or dinner, and
just being with each other. Sometimes we
talk about business, and they'll pitch in with
an idea of how it might work. Sometimes we
don't talk about business at all. I always say, if
there are five millionaires in the room, you'll
become the sixth by nature. I don't think it is
a coincidence that we have attracted the most
talented people in Qatar, and there are people
from the outside that want to join Starlink too.'

To fight a fire, light a fire

It's never easy to join a company after it has undergone
a major upheaval, and even less so following a seismic
shift. When Holly Kulka joined S&P Global Ratings in
2015, the financial industry, and especially credit ratings agencies, were still cleaning up after the wildfire
of the global financial crisis. It was a period of introspection and change at the company after they had
endured business stress, government lawsuits, repu-
tational damage and a macroeconomic meltdown.

The period that followed was a pivotal moment for
S&P Global Ratings, said Holly, who joined the firm
as its global chief risk and compliance officer in the
aftermath of this period of reckoning.

'When I came to this company, they were still
dealing with the fallout from legal action taken
by government agencies and regulators and
there were a lot of consultants and other people
telling them how to do their job. Everybody
recognised that change was necessary, but
what aspects of it, how much of it and how
it would integrate with the business was
not clear. I realised I was just another voice.
I needed to cut through all that noise and help,
instead of just adding to the stress.'

Holly and the senior team realised that they needed
to set clear priorities, but all of this was set against a
storm of new regulations on the back of the financial
crisis. Not only did S&P Global need to rebuild its reputation, but it also needed to figure out how to embed
all the necessary changes into the structure and culture
of the organisation. Describing the decision-making at
that time, Holly said:

'It was a good company. There were 100 things
we could have done, but you have to prioritise.
You have to only focus on what is important
and then move from there and iterate. If you
begin with grandiose dreams that are just too
big, you'll never be able to do anything.

'The mantra I came up with was "harmful
versus painful". We needed to deal with what
was harmful to the business. I was empathetic

about what was painful, but we had so much to do, we needed to prioritise so we could move forward as a business. We wanted to rebuild our reputation as a trusted adviser. To do this, we had to adapt to regulation from multiple angles. We needed to align our business with new regulations while also working proactively with regulators. All while building a robust risk and compliance framework. Ultimately, we all wanted the same thing: quality, transparency and customer protection.

'Part of the rebuilding process and moving forward as a business was to make sure everyone understood that what had happened did not invalidate all the good work that the company did. What we do is very important to the market and there is a lot of technology behind it, but there are human elements as well. That means there is the potential for human error. However, we were working hard to minimise the times this happened and, when they did happen, we would prioritise disclosing and fixing it over everything.'

Today, S&P Global Ratings has revenues of $3 billion and 8,000 employees around the world. It has a world-class reputation for transparency and good governance.

REFLECTIVE EXERCISE: Fire fighting

A natural response is to fight against pressure. Holly's approach was to collaborate and engage fully.

What is the fire in your situation, and what might an alternative approach look like?

What to do when your dreams don't come true

As an eight-year-old, I would often look up at the sky above, dreaming of being an astronaut. The world at that time was still enthralled by space, ever since Neil Armstrong and Buzz Aldrin had put on their bulky moon suits and taken the first steps on the Moon. It was Armstrong who had been the first to wriggle out of a small square hole in the Eagle rocket, 800 miles above the Earth's atmosphere. Once outside, he lowered a small drawbridge holding a TV camera allowing the world to see. As he backed down that ladder, 600 million people watched on TV, holding their collective breaths as they waited for him to become the first ever man on the Moon. As he stepped onto the Moon's surface, he uttered the now immortal words: 'That's one small step for man... one giant leap for mankind.'

Like almost everyone alive during that magic period, I imagined taking my own giant leaps on the lunar surface. Yet for all those millions like me, how many were successful in this endeavour? Just twelve.

The odds of walking on the Moon were (and still are) astronomically small. Being born outside the USA meant your odds were zero. If you were born outside the period 1923–1934, your odds were zero. Even as an American born in that period, the odds were approximately 1 in 235 million. If you were a woman, or non-white, too tall/small, didn't have a certain career or weren't seen as bright, your odds were zero. Even for the lucky twelve who did walk on the Moon, fate played a part. The man whose job it was to decide who would go on which missions was NASA's director of crew flight operations, Donald K 'Deke' Slayton. Deke's first choice for the first astronaut to walk on the Moon was Gus Grissom. Unfortunately, he didn't get to fulfil this honour because he died, along with his crew, in a launch pad fire eighteen months before Armstrong touched down.[107]

Many men were selected for the astronaut programme. They trained, slept and ate together for months. Their whole life was devoted to the space programme. Walking on the Moon was the pinnacle of all their ambitions, the goal they strived for day and night. Imagine, if you can, being in that group but not making it to the Moon. Dick Gordon was such a man. Gordon was the last Apollo astronaut to train extensively for lunar exploration without ever landing on the Moon. After being on the backup team for earlier flights, he flew as the Command Module Pilot of Apollo 12, the second crewed mission to the Moon. Sixty miles above the Moon he launched his two crew mates, Pete Conrad and Alan Bean, to land in the Ocean of Storms.

While orbiting above his colleagues, he took photos of potential future landing sites, one of which he believed he would eventually touch down on himself and fulfil his dream. Gordon was down to be the commander on a subsequent flight, Apollo 18, which would have meant taking the much-coveted Moonwalk. Unfortunately for him, that mission was cancelled due to budget cuts. In an extensive NASA interview in 1965, Gordon was asked how he felt about sending his crew mates to the Moon while he took photos:

> 'I was all alone. It's envy maybe, a little bit. The name of the game as far as I was concerned was to walk on the Moon. And at that time, I was relegated not to do that. And I had a job and a function to perform.'[108]

Gordon described how Al Bean had subsequently made a painting, which he called *The Fantasy*. In this painting, he had all three of the astronauts of Apollo 12 standing on the lunar surface. At the end of the interview, Gordon was asked how he wanted to be remembered. 'A contributor,' he said.

Despite failing to achieve his single most important goal, Gordon was able to reframe his experience. He recognised that he had helped others achieve his dream.[109] Gordon was a confident man. Just by being part of the lunar programme he'd proven that he was among the best of the best. Sure, he struggled with not achieving his personal ambition, but he didn't allow his ego to get in the way.

Finding this balance is not easy for a disruptive leader. Often, when individuals find themselves at the forefront of disruption, it is like a drug. The sense of being special, the 'chosen one', feeds the ego. Those who warn of threats are perceived as cynics. Those who seek to put governance in place are unnecessarily controlling. When everything crashes, those leaders can look back and blame bad luck. The reality is often that they were pig-headed, duped by their own sense of importance.

If you find yourself burned out, my heart goes out to you. But this is not the end. I have coached many founders who failed, and executives who, without warning, were let go from their roles, often having served their organisations for many years. The shock, anger and grief is real. With each of them, I use the same analogy.

Imagine being a young acorn attached to an oak tree. You enjoy the summer sun and the protection of the tree. It nourishes you, connects you to purpose and all is well within the world. Then, without warning, a wind blows and you become detached and fall from a great height. The loss is significant and painful. You feel lost, disconnected and confused. 'How could this happen to me? Why has this happened to me?' A seemingly bad situation gets worse as the summer sun is replaced by autumn winds and cold evenings. You feel utterly alone.

Just when you thought it couldn't get any worse, a squirrel picks you up, carries you far away and buries you under the earth. You can no longer see. Everything you knew and relied on is gone as winter sets in. For months, nothing happens. You can do nothing but grieve, process and reflect. You think through your past. You think about those you love, your friends, and why you did what you did. Imperceptibly at first, you start to reconnect to yourself, to what makes you, you. To your purpose, what's important to you. You start to feel more grounded, and you send down a deep root. No one else can see anything yet, but the work you are doing deep underground is critical to your next phase of growth.

Then, seemingly without warning, a new shoot breaks through. There's a difference you want to make, and you are in the best place ever to make that difference. The sun warms, the spring rains water you, and you set about your purpose with gusto.

REFLECTIVE EXERCISE: Learning from failure

Think of a crushing failure in your past. What did you learn from it?

Now more generally, consider the following questions:

1. What has failure taught you about yourself?
2. How can you reframe your experience to benefit others?
3. Are you giving yourself permission to be human, and to grieve what you've lost?

229

10
What To Do When You Get Burned (Out)

I was asked to work with the board of a charity. They had a clear purpose, thousands of willing specialist volunteers and a market needing their focus. Literally hundreds of thousands of lives depended upon their success. But there was a problem. While the CEO was a lovely, driven man, he had burned out. Making matters worse, the board was not making the tough decisions and, with no leader driving things forward, the charity was beginning to drift away from its purpose. Until something changed, there would be no disruption and people would continue to die needlessly.

The World Health Organization's International Classification of Disease (ICD-10) characterises burnout as 'a state of vital exhaustion'.[110] This was updated in ICD-11 as follows:

'Burn-out is a syndrome conceptualised as resulting from chronic workplace stress that has not been successfully managed. It is characterised by three dimensions:

1. Feelings of energy depletion or exhaustion;

2. Increased mental distance from one's job, or feelings of negativism or cynicism related to one's job; and

3. Reduced professional efficacy.'

Many leaders, particularly those with a disruptive agenda, will recognise this description. For anyone consumed with the desire to change the world, burn-out is a constant threat because the only way to grow your fire, and thus the scale of your disruption, is to increase heat, fuel and oxygen continually. That takes a lot of energy, time and commitment. We become so passionate about our cause, expending every ounce of energy and time in seeking to redress differences, that we often fail to recognise the warning signs. Even when we do, we can ignore them until it's too late. We burn out.

A Harvard Medical School study found that some 96% of senior leaders feel somewhat burned out, and a third describe their feelings of burnout as extreme.[111] While there has traditionally been a reticence to publicly announce this, because it was seen as a weakness, more leaders are coming forward to discuss this issue. Lloyds Banking Group chief António Horta-Osório was the first to speak publicly about the perils of exhaustion when he announced a two-month period of leave in 2011 due to 'extreme fatigue' from over-work. Tom Blomfield, the founder of neobank Monzo, stepped down from his position as part-time president in May 2020, saying he found it impossible to switch off. Blomfield spoke out about the myth of the super-hero boss, who sleeps just four hours a night and can effortlessly juggle the demands of wooing investors, generating revenue and managing the media, with no apparent impact on their health. 'If it is true, I've never met that person,' he said.[112]

Despite a move to be more open about the pressure leaders are under, I often find myself warning senior executives about the dangers of burnout. If they leave things too late, I say, they won't just ruin their own health, they will also jeopardise everything they've worked towards. Exhaustion means no energy; no energy means no heat; no heat means no fire. Burnout means a steady decline towards chaos and random-ness, with no worthwhile work being accomplished.

When you are in the thick of the excitement of dis-ruption, it is difficult to recognise the warning signs of burnout. Or to not dismiss them. This was the case with another leader I coached, here I'll call him Harry. Harry was in his early thirties and a rising star within a pharmaceutical company. He had been tasked with turning around a failing division and, on the face of it, was doing a fantastic job. Scratch below the surface, though, and the reality was quite different. Harry was married, with young children, and managing a commute of four hours a day. Some days he would spend the night close to the office because his long hours meant it was hardly worth making the trip home. On the days he did go home, he'd rarely get there in time to kiss his kids goodnight.

'I recognise that I can't keep working these hours, but I figure that as I am young, I need to do it now,' he told me. It was as if he'd accepted that burnout was a given, so he wanted to get ahead before he succumbed. Oh, the irony.

Burnout is not a mental illness, or caused by a single event. WHO, whose definition I quoted above, state that burnout is a process in which 'everyday stresses and anxieties gradually undermine one's mental and physical health.' Anyone in a position of leadership will recognise this scenario. Everyone wants a piece of you. Back-to-back meetings fill your calendar. Switching on your laptop triggers an avalanche of emails. Your to-do list is so long you don't even have time to read it. International responsibilities require that you be available way beyond normal office hours. Your New Year's resolution to take better care of yourself is a distant memory. Occasionally, you may find yourself doodling an addition to the never-ending to-do list: 'Research personal cloning...'

Most leaders are great at cognitive dissonance. We know we are working too hard, but we do it anyway. Eventually, though, the 'drip, drip, drip' of the demands of everyday leadership wears us down until we reach a point where our bodies (or minds) shut down in a final act of self-preservation. Believe it or not, burnout is the body's safety mechanism – a last-ditch attempt to protect us.

REFLECTIVE EXERCISE: Are you close to burnout?

Tally up whichever of the following statements apply to you:

☐ I feel wired and tired.

☐ I feel exhausted regardless of how much I sleep.

☐ My brain feels like it's in fog or cotton wool.

☐ I feel older than my age (exhaustion saps at every cell).

☐ I get a mid-morning/afternoon slump (did I eat sleeping tablets by mistake?).

☐ I need caffeine to function.

☐ I need alcohol or drugs to relax/sleep.

☐ My injuries take longer to heal.

☐ I have an irritable bowel/digestive issue (eg, IBS), food intolerances, allergies.

☐ I crave salt and sugar.

☐ I get frequent illnesses (eg, colds, flu, chest infections).

☐ I'm less resilient (I take longer to recover from setbacks, I get stressed more easily).

☐ Physical exercise wipes me out for days.

☐ I'm irritable and impatient.

☐ I have decreased energy, passion, or joy.

☐ My relationships are failing.

☐ I'm anxious, experience high levels of stress and/or depression.

☐ I want to run away or hide.

☐ I'm finding it difficult to make decisions.

Now count the number of ticks.

Even a small number of ticks should be a serious warning sign. More ticks means you are on borrowed time. If you value yourself and your loved ones, or want to achieve your purpose, act now.

Your burnout change curve

What few people in a position of leadership tend to consider is the amount of energy they are stealing from what could be a vibrant home life. The more senior you get, the more imperative it is that you take time, during your workday, to gain energy and time (E+T). It's the only way to protect yourself from burnout. This ensures not only quality thinking that helps your organisation, but also protects your health, personal relationships and quality of life. If you don't do something now, it could take you months, even years, to recover.

I speak as someone who has been there and did not seek to find that balance. Like most leaders, I was convinced I was indispensable and immune to burnout. Friends and colleagues used to question me about my hours and my workload. 'I'm fine,' I'd say. 'It's necessary.' 'I don't get stressed,' I'd add. I fully believed

I could go on like that forever. Right up until the moment I couldn't.

In the introduction I described how, in 2008, despite the calamitous global financial crash, I took a six-month sabbatical from the business I had founded, leaving my management team in charge. The truth is, I had no choice. I had reached total burnout. Six months turned into a year. I tried to go back into work as the CEO but within three days knew I hadn't recovered enough. One year turned into three. I spent a long time in therapy, trained as a psychotherapist, studied burnout and recovery and completed a master's in leadership coaching. I wanted to understand what had happened, how to recover and how I could help others avoid this.

Your willingness to make crucial changes to your routine to protect yourself from burnout will depend on where you are on your own change curve.[113]

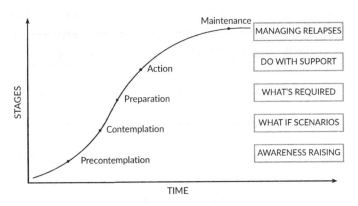

The five stages and processes of change
(Transtheoretical Model)

The following stages apply to any kind of change in our lives (personal or organisational):

1. Precontemplation

2. Contemplation

3. Preparation

4. Action

5. Maintenance

Precontemplation

At this stage, you're in denial. As far as you are concerned, there is no problem, and if there is, it is someone else's. At a push, you may accept that you are on the edge of burnout, but believe it's a temporary issue – despite the fact you've been suffering with various issues for a few years. Others can see it and might even have mentioned it, but you are having none of it. You say, 'I'm fine,' and fully believe it.

Contemplation

You have some level of recognition that there is a problem, and that you are a part of it. Typically, a move to this stage in the change curve is sparked by an intervention of some kind to raise our awareness such as feedback, coaching, a diagnostic, book, self-reflection or a trip to the doctor. We are left thinking about the impact of our behaviour, running 'what-if' scenarios in our minds and imagining what change might look like. In summary, we become more aware and begin to reflect deeply.

If, as a burnout candidate, you are reading this chapter and thinking, 'Yes, this is me,' it can feel like a light being turned on. For some, it is liberating. 'Things can change.' For others, it can feel scary. 'What does this mean?'

Preparation

As we become convinced of the need for change, we start to think about what that change should look like and formulate a plan. 'What will I do and how? What support might I need? When is the right time to implement change?'

Action

At this stage, we are actively engaged in trying to change behaviours and we need the right type of support to maximise our chances of success. Positive behavioural change takes at least six months.

Maintenance

This phase is about cementing those hard-won changes, while planning for the inevitable relapses (especially likely when we're stressed or under pressure).

Succeeding in making a deep behavioural change typically involves moving sequentially from one stage to the next. There's little likelihood we will commit to an action if we don't think we have a problem to start with. But what does preventing, or remedying, burnout look like on a practical level? It will depend upon how far down the path to burnout you are (and the sooner you stop potential burnout in its tracks, the easier it will be to deal with), but below are steps all leaders should be taking:

- Delegate or empower more
- Cut down your working hours
- Get some help
- Don't sweat the small stuff
- Take regular time off and seek to regain balance
- Rest more
- Sleep more
- Find and invest in interests outside of work
- Exercise
- Enjoy walking in nature
- Take lunch breaks
- Eat healthier
- See a doctor, coach or therapist
- Meditate
- Spend time with loved ones

- Drink less alcohol/caffeine

- Invest in yourself

- Enjoy self-awareness

- Find opportunities to give back

If, as in my case, things have gone too far, you may need to take more drastic steps. This might be taking a sabbatical and stepping aside to let someone else lead for a season. You will need to seek a place and time to reconnect to you, recover your spirit, find your difference and re-energise your soul. If you don't, things will only get worse.

REFLECTIVE EXERCISE: Preventing burnout

Consider the following:

- What do I need to do to protect myself better (and my business/family)?
- What stage of change am I at right now?
- What action will I commit to (make it specific, measurable, achievable, realistic and time-bound)?

Here are some examples of actions to take or commit to right now:

- I will take a daily lunch hour, including a twenty-minute walk, no matter what the weather, starting tomorrow. I will tell _____ and ask them to hold me accountable.

- I will book a week's holiday by the end of this week, my budget is _____. I want to go to

_____, and the dates of my holiday will be _____.

- I will sign up for coaching within the next month. I will contact _____ _____ by the end of this week.

- I recognise that I'm burned out and I need to take serious action. My action is to contact _____, now/within _____ days, and ask for help. I have put a reminder in my phone to do so.

The more energy and time you have, the more effective the heat you will bring to bear. If you do find yourself struggling, work with a good executive coach. They live and work outside of your system and can bring a great amount of external energy to bear. They also give you time to think and reflect deeply. That is a key reason why so many studies show that you can expect a minimum return on investment in coaching of 7:1.[114]

Finding balance

The phrase 'work-life balance' has become a bit of a cliché, but like so many of these oft-repeated sayings, it has significant merit. Too many leaders consider their non-work time as there to support their work life. They view evenings, weekends and holidays as a resource, essential for putting some much-needed energy back into their tanks, or as 'breathing space' to ruminate over a problem that is driving them mad. If they're lucky, they'll get back to work with just enough energy to stave off complete burnout for another week.

People in senior roles need a strong support network behind them. Some leaders can find (what at least appears to be) balance because they have an extremely supportive partner. Perhaps tellingly, it is extremely rare to find a CEO married to another CEO, or a senior executive married to another senior executive. It can be an incredibly challenging scenario because the demands of a senior (and often international) role so often require the support of the other. Ginni Rometty, the ex-IBM CEO, said that her husband had deliberately pursued a more flexible career to support her in taking the top job.[115] The pressure of a demanding role can be a challenge when both partners have careers. If one gets called up for a big opportunity, what happens to the other one? How do you balance this with your personal wellbeing? With your relationship with your partner, with your children and friends, not to mention make time for fitness, nutrition and mental health? They're all big, important parts of your life that should go hand in hand with, or at least complement, your career.

We've talked a lot about aligning purpose with disruptive leadership, and much of this flows from personal purpose. One of the questions I often get asked at a senior level is: 'How do I know what my next job should be?' Or, 'I've been approached about this specific role in this particular company – should

I take it?' I have to tell them that I don't have the answers. Much as I've tried, I'm no god. However, I do know some useful principles to apply.

Imagine setting off on a lengthy journey without a destination in mind. How would you decide when to turn left or right? Or, say you are taking a trip and like to climb mountains but also enjoy lying on the beach. You might head to the nearest mountain range, but without proper planning you could be miles away from the seaside. My estimate is that 70% of the leaders that I speak to are in a situation like this and have not properly considered their personal purpose and, therefore, their journey to fulfil it.

'What do you want to be when you grow up?' is one of those questions we were all asked as children. The truth is, very few young people are clear about what they want to do, and many of those who do will have changed their minds by the time they reach adulthood. Being open to learning and change, understanding more about who we are and the impact we want to have in the world gives us greater clues as to the kind of person we want to be and what we want to achieve (this is loosely what I refer to as your 'personal purpose'). At eight years old, I wanted to be an astronaut. At sixteen, I felt called to devote my life to God and serve the Church. By the time I'd reached my thirties, I had set my sights on becoming a successful entrepreneur within the tech world. In my forties, I retrained and switched careers and now, in my (early!) fifties, I'm the CEO of a company dedicated to supporting leaders achieving meaningful purpose, with a specific focus on equality. Aside from the early dream of becoming an astronaut, there has been a single thread that has remained constant throughout my entire life – the desire to work with others to release their potential, with a focus on leadership. That is my purpose – to help leaders achieve meaningful purpose.

REFLECTIVE EXERCISE: The wheel of life

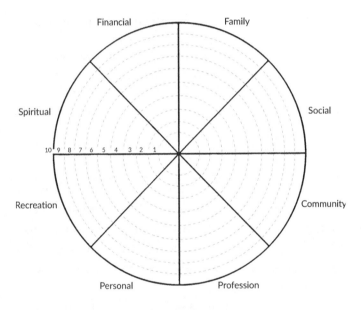

Wheel of Life

The wheel of life is a useful tool to assess and understand how balanced your life is currently. Make three copies of the wheel. On the first, give yourself a score as to where you think you are in each segment and then join the spokes of the wheel. On the second, get your partner, a colleague or friend to do the same thing, scoring you according to where they think you are. On the remaining wheel, score where you would like to be. What differences are there between the three wheels?

Spend a few hours thinking through the results. What do you want to change? What *needs* to change? The time has come to take control of your life, because the only person that can change the balance of your life is you.

Note: You can also use a similar wheel for other areas of your life or work. For business/leadership categories, try: vision, strategy, execution, sales, finance, people, development and work/life balance. Other words you can use: culture, innovation, transformation, cash, prioritisation, results, growth... The list is endless. What works for you?

If you let it, work will take every hour you have. If things need to change, you need to change them. Take control of your diary and be completely clear about what needs to be in it this week. Everything else can be stripped out. Give those tasks to someone else, or just say no.

Nearly all of the leaders I spoke to for this book insisted on ringfencing some 'me time'. They all worked ten-, even fourteen-hour days, but made sure they carved out time for friends and family. Where possible, weekends were sacrosanct. Many, such as Kathryn Dolan, the group executive and vice president of human resources at Bureau Veritas, pursues hobbies and interests far removed from her day job. She told me:

'I'm absolutely passionate about football. My family attends every home game of our local football club and I'm involved in girls' youth football. There's nothing quite like standing in the stands at the weekend, chanting for your team. It's tribal and stress relieving and something that keeps you grounded in reality. It also means your whole perspective isn't just one of being a senior person in a large corporation.

'I don't want work to be the only thing that defines me. I am quite ruthless about making sure I have clear boundaries between my work and personal life.'

REFLECTIVE EXERCISE: Who are you?

To help shape your personal and career decisions and ensure they reflect who you are, try the following exercises:

1. Rewrite your obituary (from the first exercise). No, seriously. After reading this book and digesting the ideas presented, what now would you like others to say about you? Your achievements? Your value? How you have spent your time?

2. What legacy do you want to leave within the next three years? Think about key achievements.

Write them down and then start to think of a plan for how you will achieve them. Be careful about what you write, because if you are successful these will be the headlines on your next CV/resume.

3. Make a list: what is helping you achieve your purpose, goals and objectives, and what is weighing you down? How can you remove the weights to allow you to fly?

Conclusion

Throughout this book I've used the analogy of fire to bring to life the components that good leaders need to become great. Whether you are starting out, growing or trying to protect what you have built, you will know how difficult it is to disrupt 'what is' in the pursuit of something better. By learning and applying the principles of fire, you will harness a powerful force that will enable you to achieve your goals.

We started this book by identifying how personal purpose is shaped by the difference we seek to make. The bigger the difference, the more energy you need to expend over time to bring about the change you want to see. The outcome of your effort is heat – the first element required to start a fire.

As you pursue your purpose, you draw others to your cause. Amazing human beings who willingly give their energy and time. You will also attract much-needed cash to sustain and grow. This is your fuel, the second element of your fire.

Those you want to disrupt are your target market. By building momentum, small wins become bigger wins, providing your final essential element – oxygen.

Fire = heat (energy over time) + fuel (people and cash) + oxygen (the market)

Once your fire is lit, with the right conditions and skill you can increase heat, fuel and oxygen to grow your fire. But watch out, firefighters know that losing just one of these elements means your fire will go out.

Fire is hot, uncompromising and, if left unchecked, will burn indiscriminately. Unprincipled and opportunistic leaders take advantage of this and allow their unconstrained fires to grow out of control in the pursuit of success at any cost. They may be lauded for a while, but the end result is a flashfire, or worse, a wildfire that leaves a trail of devastation and human misery. History will not treat these leaders kindly.

Instead, leaders who recognise the headwinds and act to ensure their purposeful fire remains burning are those who deserve great credit.

An example of the challenge these leaders face came nine months after the world had gone into lockdown as a result of Covid-19. I found myself speaking to the seasoned CEO of a listed heavy manufacturing company enjoying a stellar global brand. But all was not well. The pandemic had taken their customers (the oxygen from their fire), and the cash that came with it. They had already raised significant cash to stay afloat and were in the process of (successfully) raising more. Like many businesses, they were facing an existential crisis, and not just because of Covid. Short term, they didn't know how long Covid would last or how long the sector would take to recover. But longer term, the company's products relied on fossil fuels, and as he said to me 'in less than thirty years that will no longer be an option.'

This would be a great case study for an aspiring MBA student. But in this case, the need was real, current and pressing.

Added into the mix was the workforce; typical of heavy manufacturing, it had a strong engineering base, with most employees having worked for the company for decades. Ask any leader who has sought to transform such an organisation (think back to the energy required to change the employee terms of a heavily unionised rail company), and they will tell you how difficult the journey is.

What had been a roaring fire was now at risk of being extinguished.

'Mark, even if we survive, we have no cash for serious technology development. What do we do?'

What would you say?

Every time I'm asked a question like this, I'm very conscious that I know nothing. But what I do believe I can do is ask some questions. Questions which are premised on the framework I've outlined within this book.

- **HEAT:** What's your personal purpose? What's the difference you seek to bridge? Equally, what is the company's purpose? Do you have the (requisite) energy and time to pursue that difference? What are the values you live by? What is the quality of your leadership and where are the gaps? What level of thinking are you operating at?

- **FUEL:** Are you communicating the difference you seek (your purpose) to everyone? How are you engaging your people in your purpose, and what do you need to do to ensure you have the right people? This includes your leadership team, bench strength and expertise, and the right culture. Cash wise – what do you need? Do you have enough? How will you sustain cash over the short, medium and long term? What can you do differently?

- **OXYGEN:** The key to staying relevant is meeting your market's needs. Focus your communications around your purpose and ensure you connect at an emotive level. Watch out for headwinds and wind changes, and find strategies that fan your flames. As the common refrain says, 'Change is here to stay'. If our purpose is meaningful enough our strategy to achieve it needs to change with the prevailing conditions.

At the conclusion of our conversation, it was clear the gap was around how to transition the company.

I reminded him that however desperate he might feel, he had a clear personal and company purpose, he had a global brand, and despite his current predicament the company had more money than most startups. On top of that he had world-class engineering expertise and a supply chain the envy of the world. What felt like an existential crisis could be the very thing that ignited the company's bold new future. What was required was to ask the right questions (see section on Level Three thinking). As I've said previously, finding the right questions is hard. Answering them even harder. But unless energy and time are devoted to Level Three thinking, sooner or later, your competitors will gain advantage, and you risk going into administration and/or being subject to a fire sale.

As a small but growing company you might feel big corporates have it easy. The reality is very different. Their scale might be larger, giving them certain advantages, but at any moment the wind can, and will, change. Making an entrepreneurial pivot is far harder for an established company than a more agile one.[116]

To ensure your fire is a force for positive change, whilst protecting yourself and others, quality leadership is critical. Leading with purpose, adherence to lived values and continuous personal development will help you shape the direction and type of fire you build. Great leaders bring out the best in others and build cultures of sustained competitive advantage.

Once your fire is burning, you will need to protect it from those who would seek to disrupt you. Remember, they need only to lower your heat, steal your fuel or starve you of oxygen to succeed. If we are not careful, we can become trapped within a closed system and allow our heat to dissipate as a result of entropy (a slide into chaos or disorder). Ensuring long-term sustainable competitive advantage requires that we build a learning organisation – one that continually disrupts itself by challenging the status quo, internally and externally. Such an organisation requires a culture that moves beyond Level One safety thinking ('Are we getting it right?') and even Level Two thinking ('Are we doing the right thing?') and instead is constantly asking itself the altogether more difficult, Level Three question: 'How do we decide what's right?' Only great leaders operate with Level Three thinking, and it requires consistency of effort towards gaining diverse sources of external energy and time to think. Operating at this level also ensures focus on your personal life. It is easy to burn out. Prioritising personal energy and time (how you use it and how you gain it) is essential.

Anyone, anywhere, can make a difference. Forget about the cult-like status afforded to well-known leaders, as comparisons will do you no favours. The reality is that each of us is human, with unique superpowers and our own Kryptonite. You will know failure. You may burn out. But each of us can always take time out to re-engage with our purpose to make a difference to others.

Now ask yourself how you would rate your own leadership? Your levels of energy? Are you starting or growing your fire? Is your focus on protecting it?

Do you have enough fuel? What threatens your oxygen? How will history judge you?

If you took the time to complete the reflective exercises in this book, you will have taken away significant learning and action points. Now it's time to do something with them. You picked up this book for a reason. A desire to lead change, to disrupt and to make a difference. You don't need to be superhuman. Instead, focus on the difference you want to make. Use your energy and time purposefully. Protect and develop yourself. Grow those you are responsible for. Use these insights, re-visit them and make them your own.

If you need a hand, a sounding board, or you simply want to share your journey, reach out to me – I'm here. I want to help fan the flames of purposeful sustainable disruption within you. Watch out, too, for my upcoming leadership retreats. If you are striving to make a difference, or an organisation seeking to unlock the competitive advantage to be gained from improving its gender equality, consider joining WeQual.

We're in this together. The world needs leaders like you to make a difference in every sphere of society. Whether it's by bringing a smile to one child's face, or finding solutions to global issues, let's light up the world with our purposeful fires. Let's bring about the difference we need, disrupting the rancid status quo wherever we find it. Together, let's leave a lasting legacy we can be proud of.

Afterword: What Fire Are You Building?

Doing anything worthwhile requires effort, and effort is energy over time. This book is a good example. Back in 2018 I found myself tired and penniless after leaving another startup. Despite my exhaustion, I wanted a unique and fresh way to work with and support senior leaders. I gave myself permission to take time out, regardless of financial pressure, which allowed me to recharge, recover and reconnect with my purpose. I allowed myself the much-needed time to gain fresh outside-in energy through resting and meditation. It takes time to build up energy. Energy and time are closely interlinked. Taking that time and being open, sparked the insights presented in this book.

Meeting Katie Litchfield, founder of WeQual, and deciding to grow a business together has led us on an extraordinary journey. Since 2020, in our drive to achieve gender equality at the top of the world's largest organisations, we've had the extraordinary privilege to find, get to know, support, coach, champion and celebrate many of the world's top female leaders. In the process, we have built great relationships with their organisations and CEOs.

My first book draft sat for a long time on my digital shelf gathering digital dust, but my fire was building. As WeQual has continued to grow, I've had the extraordinary privilege of coaching hundreds of outstanding leaders at VP and C-suite levels (80% of them women) across the globe.

In 2022, I asked just a handful of leaders whether they would be open to being interviewed for the book and was humbled by the response. At this point my ghost writer took over and skilfully weaved their interviews into the narrative. Circa 50% of my original writing was removed, yet the core analogy of fire remains the same.

I've found that the insight I gained in 2018 holds true regardless of sector, function or culture, and regardless of whether you are working in a startup or a globally listed organisation. The greater the change you want to bring about, the more energy and time you will need, and the more heat, fuel and oxygen. It is our purpose (vision, mission, the change we want to see) that shapes the direction and size of our fire; and it is the values we hold dear (what we do, not what we say) that define whether our fire causes harm, or good. Mature servant leadership wins in the long term over opportunistic, narcissistic leaders.

You may be one of those leaders who has a deep internal fire that has been burning for years. Whether due to nature, or nurture, you are driven to bring about transformational change – to disrupt what is, for what could be. Your passion invites others to join you in a purposeful journey, attracting cash as you go in order to impact the world in some important way. Or you may find yourself seemingly thrust into a leadership position, responding to the situation you find yourself in. You are likely unseen by wider society, yet, without people like you, the world would be unrecognisable. You may think of yourself as insignificant, yet through persistence and a desire to do good you bring about transformation in those you lead, and in the environment you work within. Every sphere of our society has heroes like you.

Disruptors come in all shapes and sizes, and the vast majority are unknown. Elon Musk is rightly lauded for his approach to space, but what of the HR manager who ensures that a workplace is psychologically safe? What of the schoolteacher who instils self-belief into an eight-year-old? The charity worker who saves a family from starvation? The small startup using AI to detect early cancer? All of these are leaders and they all tap into the same components of disruption as those who become household names.

Throughout this book, we have seen examples of hugely damaging wildfires. When corporate wildfires surge without restraint, destruction follows. Yes, for a while they may be seen as 'the' business to get into but indiscriminate growth, at any cost, without consideration of ethics or morals, ends badly. When wildfires die out, which they inevitably do, the cost is incalculable. Jobs, savings, pensions, houses, relationships and health are all impacted. In the case of the 2008 crash, whole countries and populations were affected – and are still feeling those effects. For some, it is literally a matter of life and death. As such, it is incumbent upon you as a leader to stay humble, commit to personal development and surround yourself with strong characters able to limit your failures while staying true to a purposeful mission and lived values.

I believe there is a common fallacy, and one that I often buy into myself, that leaders are a breed apart. That they are somehow special; that they have superpowers, are able to achieve what mere mortals can't. I remember the first WeQual Awards finalist (a senior vice president) I coached from an international chemical company. I was a little nervous – here was a formidable woman who had succeeded in an incredibly tough and male-dominated environment. Yet due to a reorganisation, she had been let go after years of loyal and dedicated service. What could I teach her? I hadn't lived her life. But of course, in that instance, all anyone needs is reassurance, especially after being forced out of a place you'd given blood, sweat and tears to. Like anyone would be, she was navigating feelings of hurt, daze, loss and grief.

Having now coached many thousands of leaders, from startups to the CEOs of globally listed organisations, the thing that always amazes me is how alike we all are. We are all human, with doubts, fears and uncertainties. And yet, there is a will, a desire, a grit, a determination to make a difference. There is also a deep commitment to learning. I will never forget my first coaching session with an incredibly distinguished and proven global CEO. His company was about to acquire a very large organisation, and with pen in hand he asked me, 'Mark, what is it I need to watch for as we bring together these two large organisations?' Though I was tempted to crack a joke about the last time I had merged two multibillion-dollar organisations, I calmly replied, 'I can't speak from experience, but I can speak to principles and ask you some questions.' On reflection, it was his humility in asking me the question at all that has stuck with me. His openness to learning, without pride, has helped him shape the company to be the market leader. We all have something to learn from that approach.

World-changers don't just sit on the sidelines. They don't have cast-iron confidence. They are not superheroes able to turn back time. They struggle speaking. Find it hard to prioritise. Feel that they are failing their families. Don't exercise enough. Are unsure at key moments. Some are driven, 'type A' personalities – the ones who received all A-grades at school and college, were the captains of their sports teams, came first in every competitive situation. Others were invisible at school, the idea of being a captain revulsed them and they failed at college. And yet they persevered. I have found that courage is more important than confidence. Resilience is better than brilliance. A desire to make a difference is more important than ego.

Focus on the change you want to make. Prioritise yourself (starting with your energy and time). Take action. Don't allow your human frailties to stop you. Keep going and, as you do, you will start to generate heat. Your commitment will start to draw resources to you – cash, and great people. As you set about making your change, you will affect the market/environment, bringing much-needed customers and building a community. Stay focused on your purpose. Keep topping up your energy and time. Take every opportunity to develop yourself. Together, let's make the world a better place for all.

But what if you feel you've made it? You've achieved your purpose? I both congratulate you, and ask why your purpose was so small?

Liu Chuanzhi, the founder of Lenovo, the world's largest PC maker, said, 'Being a good entrepreneur doesn't just mean running your business well. A real leader should also care about society and bear more social responsibility.'[117] He goes on to mention his respect for Microsoft's Bill Gates as a particular example of this. Bill and his ex-wife Melinda Gates are not alone in their philanthropy. Many others also devote their energy and time to global concerns, often well before building personal wealth.

Within the WeQual Awards nomination process, we ask those C-suite minus one women leaders to explain what they are doing to support underrepresented minorities within their companies. Their answers often include setting up programmes to help those usually excluded from the workforce and those who are underrepresented within the workforce. It's just one of the aspects that make those women in the WeQual Awards finals so amazing – not only are they proven in their field, they also actively champion and support greater equality within and outside of their organisations.

As I've mentioned elsewhere in the book, my experience has shown me that CEOs from India have a different perspective from many CEOs in the West. When they are interviewing the finalists for the WeQual Awards, they often ask the question, 'How are you giving back?' or, 'What are you doing for your community?'

Warren Buffett has pledged that more than 99% of his wealth will go to philanthropy during his lifetime or at death, and to date has given away just over half of his Berkshire Hathaway shares.[118] He has encouraged others to do the same and, to date, hundreds of billionaires have signed up to the Warren Buffett Pledge. Each of them has committed to giving a minimum of 50% of their wealth to philanthropic causes by, or upon, their death.

Yet regardless of how much money we are worth, we all have a unique opportunity to give back. To support others. To help address the ills that plague our society. We have big problems to solve. Whether we do so through our work, or through what we give back, it is incumbent on us to either lead positive change, or to support those who are.

Are you lighting the fire within others? Providing their fuel? I hope so.

Contributors

This book wouldn't have been possible without the following interviewees, who have generously allowed their experiences and insights to be included here for us all to learn from. Below is some information about each of them and their impressive professional roles and achievements to date.

Krista Bourne, Chief Operating Officer of the Verizon Consumer Group

Krista leads a distributed team of tens of thousands of passionate employees who serve more than 110 million customers and help deliver more than $100 billion in annual revenue. During her more than twenty years with Verizon, Krista has focused on providing extraordinary customer experiences across several parts of the business. She has held various positions of increasing responsibility including director roles in customer service and retail sales, regional president, market president and SVP and president of sales and operations, where she helped shape the Verizon Consumer strategy.

She has been recognised with a WeQual Award for her outstanding career contribution and potential future impact and currently serves on the board of Dress For Success Worldwide.

Abu Bundu-Kamara, Senior Director, Global Inclusion and IBGs/Communities at Expedia Group

An accomplished strategist and change agent, Abu excels in inspiring leaders and businesses to adapt to the modern marketplace. With over twenty years of expertise in leadership, strategy and human resources, Abu is deeply committed to integrating diversity and inclusion into decision-making. Appointed as Senior Director, Global Inclusion and IBGs at Expedia in 2021, Abu oversees efforts outside the United States, promoting inclusive practices. Abu also actively contributes to various organisations focused on inclusion, holds positions on the boards of Catalyst and NCTJ, and regularly speaks at conferences, sharing insights from a career spanning global brands like Pearson and *The Economist*.

Daniela Cachich, President of the
Beyond CO Business Unit, Ambev

Daniela currently leads the portfolio of alcoholic beverages Beyond Beer, as well as non-alcoholic beverages, at Ambev. Previously, Daniela led PepsiCo Foods Brazil as CMO for almost five years, where she was responsible for the snacks brands portfolio. Daniela has spent more than twenty years working in leading consumer goods companies, accumulating experience in building and developing categories and in innovation. She is a member of the Advisory Board of Grupo Boticário, the biggest beauty company in the world, and Instituto FreeFree, a social organisation that works in cycles of freedom for girls and women who have suffered violence. She also serves as a member of Insper's Marketing Board.

Daniela was on *Forbes'* list of the '20 Most Influential Women in Brazil' and the 'Best CMOs in Brazil' in 2020.

Steve Cahillane, Chairman, President and CEO,
Kellanova (formerly Kellogg Company)

Steve Cahillane joined Kellogg Company in October 2017 as chief executive officer, and became chairman of the board in March 2018. Prior to Kellogg, in 2014, Steve assumed the role of president and chief executive officer at The Nature's Bounty Co, the largest global pure-play manufacturer, marketer and speciality retailer of health and wellness products. Prior to this, he spent seven years with the Coca-Cola Company and eight years with AB InBev, the world's largest brewing company.

He currently serves on the Northwestern University Board of Trustees, The Consumer Goods Forum Board of Directors, the Smithsonian National Board, the Colgate-Palmolive Board of Directors and as co-trustee of the WK Kellogg Foundation Trust. Steve holds a Bachelor of Arts degree in political science from Northwestern University and a Master of Business Administration degree from Harvard University.

Mark Cutifani, Chief Executive at Anglo American and Chair at Total

Born and raised in Wollongong, Australia, Mark Cutifani began his career working in the coal mines in his hometown while completing a degree in mining engineering. Since then, he has led some of the largest mining projects and companies across six continents, producing more than thirty mineral products.

In his eighteen years as a chief executive of three different mining groups, he has built a unique track record for leading significant change in safety and health, environment and social performance. His work in these areas has been recognised by the Thomas Edison Global Innovation Awards for Collaborative change, as a 'Technoserve 50th Anniversary Honouree', in recognition of 'extraordinary leadership in creating sustainable business solutions to end poverty around the world', and more recently as Europe's most sustainable mining leader. He has also been recognised in Australia with the AusIMM Institute Medal and in South Africa with the Brigadier Stokes Award, in both cases the highest recognition by industry colleagues, for his contribution to the global mining industry. He is also a past president of the ICMM, based in London.

Heather Cykoski, Senior Vice President Industrial and Process Automation, Schneider Electric

Having joined ABB in 2005 and assuming various leadership roles, Heather played a pivotal role in accelerating new growth for the organisation. She spearheaded ABB's global efforts in developing, implementing and managing relationships, overseeing total business acquisition worldwide, and leading the global engineering, procurement and construction Industry business. Over her more than two-decade-long career, Heather demonstrated her prowess as a passionate global business leader, guiding multi-divisional, multi-cultural teams in the energy value chain.

In recognition of her outstanding contributions, Heather earned the title of Gamechanger Progress Champion in both 2023 and 2022. Her leadership excellence was further acknowledged with the WeQual Americas Leadership Excellence award in 2021. Notably, in the same year, she received accolades as a Global Leader of Influence in World Affairs, was recognized as one of the 10 Most Aspiring Women Leaders of 2021, and featured among the Influential Women in Technology 2020 list.

In August 2023, Heather joined Schneider Electric as Senior Vice President Industrial and Process

Automation, North American Operations. She also is a member of the global executive leadership team.

Heather's commitment to fostering diversity and inclusion is evident in her involvement in various initiatives. She was a member of the McKinsey and Company, Advancing Women Executives in Energy 2021 Cohort, served as the Society of Women Engineers (SWE) Executive and SWE Local Raleigh Chapter Keynote, chaired the Mozambique, Africa Doyenne Initiative, and contributed as a member of the Texas A&M Alumni and Society of Petroleum Engineers. Additionally, she served on the Aspen Institute of Economy, Society and Environment, held roles as the Encompass D&I Chairman, and was a Division D&I board member.

Beyond her professional endeavors, Heather dedicated her time to serving on the Board of Fluitron LLC and the World Affairs Council of Greater Houston.

Kathryn Dolan, Group Executive and Vice President Human Resources, Bureau Veritas

Kathryn Dolan joined Bureau Veritas, a French-listed global professional services company employing over 80,000 people, in 2017 and led HR for Europe before her appointment in 2022 to the Group Executive Committee.

Prior to joining Bureau Veritas, Kathryn's career spanned various global multinational organisations across different market sectors. Kathryn began her career at Deloitte. From 2003 to 2017, she held a number of positions at Fujitsu, a global information and communication technology provider. Her roles included director of organisational effectiveness; HR director EMEA; and, operationally, client service improvement lead.

Kathryn holds an MSc in organisation and business psychology from the University of Liverpool and a degree in economics from the University of Manchester. Notably, she became a Fellow of the Chartered Institute of Personnel and Development, is a qualified leadership coach and non-executive director. Outside of her professional career, Kathryn is an ambassador for increasing participation in girls' youth football.

Munera Al Dosari, CEO, Starlink

Munera Al Dosari is a renowned business leader and entrepreneur, currently serving as the CEO of Starlink Qatar, part of the Ooredoo Group. With her expertise in business planning, strategy creation, financial control and telecom engineering, she has been instrumental in the growth and success of Starlink Qatar. Munera also sits on Palestine's Ooredoo Board of Directors. She co-founded Airlift systems, a logistics and transportation company, and invested in Angel.qa, a startup accelerator that supports early-stage tech companies.

Her core values and principles centre on innovation, integrity and perseverance. Her passion for technology, the economy and politics is evident in her work. She enjoys taking on challenging environments and believes in positively impacting society through her work and empowering women to succeed in the industry. Munera was recognised with the Talent of the Year Award at the Arab Women Awards in 2014 and was named a WeQual EMEA winner in 2020. She is also a graduate of the Qatar Leadership Center Class of Harvard 2013.

Jasi Halai, Chief Operating Officer, 3i

Jasi Halai joined 3i in 2005 and has held a variety of posts, most recently as the group financial controller and chief operating officer. She was appointed to the board in 2022 and is a member of the Executive, Investment, Group Risk and ESG Committees. Prior to joining 3i, she worked for CDC Group (now British International Investment) and at Actis.

Jasi is a non-executive director at Barratt Developments PLC and was previously a non-executive director at Porvair Plc. She is a Chartered Management Accountant and holds an MSc in investment management from the CASS Business School.

Tim Harrison, Managing Director, Harrison Family Vets

Tim graduated from the LSE in 1992 with an MSc in HR. His first professional role was as a personnel manager for an international electronics distributor. A role in general management within the distribution sector followed. In 1995 Tim joined White Cross Vets to oversee the business side of his father's practice in Leeds. In 2000, Tim co-founded Vets4Pets, a national chain of franchised practices. In 2005, Mars Inc appointed Tim as the general manager at Banfield International, overseeing all Mars' veterinary interests outside of the USA, including business development work throughout Latin America, Japan, China and Europe.

In 2008, Tim returned to the UK to oversee the expansion of White Cross Vets throughout the North and Midlands. White Cross Vets was successfully sold to private equity acquirers in 2018. In 2021, Tim established Harrison Family Vets, an expanding chain of practices across England. Tim resides with his family in North Yorkshire and is rarely seen without his beloved whippet.

Holly Kulka, Global Chief Risk and Compliance Officer, S&P Global Ratings

Holly leads the globally integrated risk and compliance teams at S&P, including the criteria and model validation groups, managing relationships with more than twenty regulators around the world. She is a member of the S&P Global Ratings Operating Committee and is chair of the board of CRISIL Ratings.

Previously, Holly served as executive vice president, deputy general counsel for Intercontinental Exchange Inc, which acquired NYSE Euronext. As a member of the executive leadership team, she was responsible for regulatory strategy, litigation, investigations, antitrust, insurance, privacy and human resource legal matters. Before that, she was a partner at the law firm of Heller Ehrman LLP. Earlier in her career, Holly was a federal prosecutor.

Holly holds a JD from the University of Chicago and a BA from Williams College.

Katie Litchfield, Founder, WeQual

Katie Litchfield has been at the vanguard of the campaign to create gender equality in the biggest businesses in the world. This is a mission that the company she founded, WeQual, has made incredible inroads into. Katie's drive, alongside her enthusiasm, persistence and engagement, has given her an impressive and unparalleled network of global CEOs and leaders all committed to building a better business world.

As the face of WeQual, Katie also presents her own podcast in which she gets inside the heads of world business leaders, giving an instructive and unique insight into how to lead. Prior to setting up WeQual, Katie was an executive at *The Financial Times*, running their much-lauded forum events, and founded the FT Women's Forum, which proved the inspiration for WeQual's formation.

Christina Montgomery, Chief Privacy and Trust Officer, IBM

Christina oversees IBM's global privacy programme, policies, compliance and strategy. She also chairs IBM's AI Ethics Board, a multi-disciplinary team responsible for the governance of AI and emerging technologies. Christina has served in various roles at IBM, including corporate secretary to the board of directors.

A global leader in AI ethics and governance, Christina is a member of the US Chamber of Commerce AI Commission, and the United States' National AI Advisory Committee (NAIAC), established in 2022 to advise the US President and the National AI Initiative Office on a range of topics related to AI. Christina is an advisory board member of the Future of Privacy Forum (FPF), advisory council member of the Center for Information Policy Leadership (CIPL) and a member of the Women Leading Privacy Advisory Board for the International Association of Privacy Professionals (IAPP). She has a BA from Binghamton University and a JD from Harvard Law School.

Hina Nagarajan, MD and CEO, Diageo India

Hina Nagarajan is a member of the Diageo Global Executive Committee and is the managing director and CEO of Diageo India. Her key responsibilities include managing the listed company in India, growth acceleration, P&L delivery, investment, category and whitespace entry strategies, transforming consumer insight and innovation, ESG, digitalisation of the organisation as well as corporate governance and compliance. Hina also sits on the Steerco of the Diageo global digital transformation initiative. Previously, she was the managing director of Africa Emerging Markets (AEM) for Diageo, leading business operations across Ghana, Ethiopia, Cameroon, Indian Ocean, Angola and other WACA countries. Under her leadership, AEM transformed to become a significant growth driver.

Hina has spent over thirty years in the FMCG industry and held several leadership positions at Reckitt (Greater China, Malaysia and Singapore) and in India at Mary Kay, ICI Paints and Nestlé. A strong advocate of creating opportunities for women, Hina contributes to inclusion and diversity programmes. She is a member of the Board of Governors of the Advertising Standards Council of India and has served on the National Board of AmCham in India. She was also appointed as an independent non-executive director to the board of BP PLC in 2023.

Hina has an MBA from the Indian Institute of Management, Ahmedabad.

Wan Norashikin Mohd Nasir, Global Vice President of Risk Management and Business Continuity Management, Indorama Ventures

'Nonie' is an experienced strategic leader offering specialised risk management support to leading multinational corporations for the past twenty-five years. She began as a management associate in CITIGROUP and later joined PETRONAS, holding various positions from risk analyst to strategic planning, spanning almost a decade in international operations.

At PETRONAS, she held multiple leadership roles in which she introduced innovative approaches to emerging risks, supply chain BCM for refining/trading, petrochemical and marketing, and advised the executive committee and leadership teams. In 2020 she joined Indorama Ventures PCL, a global petrochemical company with over fifteen business verticals. In her current role, Nonie leads a diverse global team overseeing 147 plants in thirty-eight countries across six continents. She is also chairman of the Risk Management Council, Diversity and Inclusion Committee and is a member and secretariat to the Sustainability ESG Council.

Nonie won the APAC WeQual Leadership Excellence Award 2021, is a certified DRI Associate Business Continuity Practitioner and has a bachelor's degree in chemical engineering from UCL. She is passionate about helping people in need, stepping outside of her comfort zone, taking on new challenges and exploring new perspectives for growth. Her mantra is 'seize the day' – she believes that we don't have to wait to be confident, 'just do it' and confidence will follow.

Tom Pereira, Chief Financial Officer, MILKRUN

Tom is the CFO and member of the executive leadership team at MILKRUN, one of Australia's fastest-growing startups, backed by prominent global VC firms including Tiger Global. Tom previously spent nearly eight years at Just Eat Takeaway.com, one of the world's largest online food delivery platforms, as group finance director and member of the executive committee, overseeing a finance team of approximately 350 people in twenty countries.

Joining Takeaway.com in 2014, Tom was part of the core team that delivered the Dutch firm's 2016 IPO and subsequent acquisitions of London-listed Just Eat PLC and Nasdaq-listed Grubhub Inc. Before this, Tom spent seven years working for the CFO services practice of Deloitte Consulting in Australia and the Netherlands.

Kate Ringrose, CFO, Centrica

Kate Ringrose has gathered a wealth of energy, finance and leadership experience over seventeen years at Centrica, a large UK-based energy utility company, culminating in becoming the group chief financial officer.

Prior to joining Centrica, Kate qualified as a Chartered Accountant and Chartered Financial Analyst, training with KPMG South Africa, before relocating to the UK where she specialised in financial services audit, consulting and transaction services support.

Srimathi Shivashankar, Corporate VP and Global Head, EdTech Business, HCL Technologies

Srimathi Shivashankar is responsible for HCL's EdTech Business, which provides talent transformational services through innovative learning and assessments, products and solutions. In her previous role, Srimathi was the director of the New Vistas programme and was responsible for strategising and operationalising new HCLTech delivery centres in global talent hubs. She was also the architect of the diversity and sustainability practices, HCL Foundation and HCL Grant.

She holds a bachelor's degree in computer science and engineering from the National Institute of Technology, Tiruchirappalli, which has recognised her accomplishments through the Distinguished Alumna Award, and an MBA in International Business

Management from Ohio University. She won the WeQual Award in 2021 in the Business Transformation category and was named among the Top 25 Women Leaders in Consulting for 2023 by the Consulting Report. Srimathi has been a key speaker at various international forums such as the UN, WBCSD, World Investment Forum, WEF, NASSCOM and CII.

Jean-Pascal Tricoire, Chairman and CEO, Schneider Electric

As the head of what is the global leader in the digital transformation of energy management and automation, Jean-Pascal is committed to creating a more sustainable and inclusive future for all, using technologies and digital innovation to empower people to make the most of their energy and resources.

Jean-Pascal is a director of the worldwide board of the UN Global Compact, a UN #HeForShe Corporate IMPACT champion and a member of the International Business Council of the World Economic Forum.

Notes

1 K Litchfield, 'Tackling gender parity at the top of the world's largest companies', TEDx Talks (28 June 2022), www.youtube.com/watch?v=N10q_xvZSXM, accessed August 2023

2 GA Moore, *Crossing the Chasm: Marketing products to mainstream customers* (Harper Collins, 2014)

3 D Barufaldi, 'Warren Buffett's bear market maneuvers', *Investopedia* (25 June 2023), www.investopedia.com/articles/stocks/09/buffett-bear-market-strategies.asp, accessed August 2023

4 'The Top 25 Women Leaders in Consulting for 2022', *The Consulting Report* (16 February 2022), www.theconsultingreport.com/the-top-25-women-leaders-in-consulting-for-2022; and 'The Top 25 Women Leaders in Consulting for 2023', *The Consulting Report*, www.theconsultingreport.com/the-top-25-women-leaders-in-consulting-for-2023, both accessed August 2023

5 Other sources of fuel could include customers, partners, suppliers, the community and any other body or agency who, by expending their energy, helps you succeed. For the purposes of this chapter though, we will focus on people and cash.

6   E O'Boyle and A Mann, 'American workplace changing at a dizzying pace', Gallup (15 February 2017), www.gallup. com/workplace/236282/american-workplace-changing-dizzying-pace.aspx, accessed July 2023

7   A Suellentrop and EB Bauman, 'How influential is a good manager?', Gallup (2 June 2021), www.gallup.com/cliftonstrengths/en/350423/influential-good-manager. aspx, accessed August 2023

8   DL Stoewen, 'Suicide in veterinary medicine: Let's talk about it', *The Canadian Veterinary Journal*, 56/1 (2015), 89–92, www.ncbi.nlm.nih.gov/pmc/articles/PMC4266064, accessed August 2023

9   R Rose, 'Should I stay or should I go: Why veterinary team members leave veterinary practices', Catalyst (2018), www.isvma.org/wp-content/uploads/2018/10/ShouldIStayorShouldIGo.pdf, accessed August 2023

10 J Harter, 'Dismal employee engagement is a sign of global mismanagement', Gallup (2017), www.gallup.com/workplace/231668/dismal-employee-engagement-sign-global-mismanagement.aspx, accessed July 2023

11 Kenexa, The Many Contexts of Employee Engagement: A 2012/2013 Kenexa Work Trends Report (Kenexa High Performance Institute, 2012)

12 There are a myriad of studies and organisations, such as Gallup, Kenexa and CEB focusing on engagement research. See, for example, Corporate Leadership Council, *Driving Performance and Retention through Employee Engagement* (Corporate Executive Board, 2004), www.stcloudstate.edu/humanresources/_files/documents/supv-brown-bag/employee-engagement.pdf, accessed August 2023

13 R Scott, 'Employee engagement vs employee experience', *Forbes* (4 May 2017), www.forbes.com/sites/causeintegration/2017/05/04/employee-engagement-vs-employee-experience, accessed August 2023

14 Not a recommended team-building exercise!

15 '25 people to blame for the financial crisis', *Time* (no date), https://content.time.com/time/specials/packages/article/0,28804,1877351_1877350_1877326,00.html, accessed August 2023

16 B McLean and P Elkind, *The Smartest Guys in the Room: The amazing rise and scandalous fall of Enron* (Penguin, 2004)

17   SA Rosenthal and TL Pittinsky, 'Narcissistic leadership',
     The Leadership Quarterly, 17/6 (2006), 617–633, https://doi.
     org/10.1016/j.leaqua.2006.10.005, accessed August 2023
18   M Maccoby, 'Narcissistic Leaders: The incredible pros, the
     inevitable cons', *Harvard Business Review* (January 2004,
     reprint from January 2000 issue), 78: 69–77, https://hbr.
     org/2004/01/narcissistic-leaders-the-incredible-pros-the-
     inevitable-cons, accessed September 2023
19   W Mischel, 'Toward a cognitive social learning
     reconceptualization of personality', *Psychological Review*
     (1973), 80: 252–283, https://doi.org/10.1037/h0035002
20   M Maccoby, 'Narcissistic Leaders: The incredible pros, the
     inevitable cons', *Harvard Business Review* (January 2004,
     reprint from January 2000 issue), 78: 69–77, https://hbr.
     org/2004/01/narcissistic-leaders-the-incredible-pros-the-
     inevitable-cons, accessed September 2023
21   ME Biery, 'Private companies pull economy along',
     Forbes (1 October 2012), www.forbes.com/sites/
     sageworks/2012/10/01/private-companies-pull-economy-
     along/#144f14aa2723, accessed July 2023
22   E Musk (@elonmusk), 'The reality is great highs…', tweet
     (30 July 2017), https://twitter.com/elonmusk/status/8917
     10778205626368?lang=en, accessed July 2023
23   N Ahmed and S Bakewell, 'Tesla's burning through
     nearly half a million dollars every hour', Bloomberg
     (21 November 2017), www.bloomberg.com/news/
     articles/2017-11-21/tesla-is-blowing-through-8-000-every-
     minute-amid-model-3-woes, accessed July 2023
24   D Gelles, JB Stewart, J Silver-Greenberg and K Kelly, 'Elon
     Musk details the "excruciating" personal toll of Tesla
     turmoil', *The New York Times* (16 August 2018), www.
     nytimes.com/2018/08/16/business/elon-musk-interview-
     tesla.html, accessed July 2023
25   A Huffington, 'An open letter to Elon Musk', Thrive Global
     (17 August 2018), https://thriveglobal.com/stories/open-
     letter-elon-musk, accessed July 2023
26   E Musk (@elonmusk), 'Ford @ Tesla are the only
     2 American car companies to avoid bankruptcy…', tweet
     (19 August 2018), https://twitter.com/elonmusk/status/10
     31111742103814144?lang=en, accessed July 2023
27   A Molinsky, 'Being a Successful Entrepreneur Isn't Only
     About Having the Best Ideas', *Harvard Business Review*

(30 August 2016), https://hbr.org/2016/08/being-a-successful-entrepreneur-isnt-only-about-having-the-best-ideas, accessed September 2023

28 'Carillion: Six charts that explain what happened', BBC News (19 January 2018), www.bbc.com/news/uk-42731762, accessed August 2023

29 L Booth, 'Lessons from the collapse of Carrillion', House of Commons Library (9 July 2018), https://commonslibrary.parliament.uk/research-briefings/cdp-2018-0177, accessed July 2023

30 10 hilariously stupid products everyone knew would fail, and then they did', IQFY (no date), https://iqfy.com/stupid-products-everyone-knew-would-fail, accessed September 2023 and C Johnson, 'How to Identify an Innovative Idea', Carla Johnson (1 March 2022), www.carlajohnson.co/how-to-identify-an-innovative-idea, accessed September 2023

31 K Taylor, 'McDonald's is bringing back one of its most expensive failures – with one major difference', *Business Insider India* (2 January 2018), www.businessinsider.in/mcdonalds-is-bringing-back-one-of-its-most-expensive-failures-but-theres-a-catch/articleshow/62343494.cms, accessed August 2023; D Gellene, 'McDonald's income flat despite Arch Deluxe blitz', *Los Angeles Times* (19 July 1996), www.latimes.com/archives/la-xpm-1996-07-19-fi-25637-story.html, accessed August 2023

32 A Carr, 'The Inside Story Of Jeff Bezos's Fire Phone Debacle', Fast Company (6 January 2015), www.fastcompany.com/3039887/under-fire, accessed August 2023

33 J Harter, 'Employee engagement on the rise in the U.S.', *Gallup News* (26 August 2018), https://news.gallup.com/poll/241649/employee-engagement-rise.aspx, accessed August 2023

34 Kotter, 'Does corporate culture drive financial performance?', *Forbes* (10 February 2011), www.forbes.com/sites/johnkotter/2011/02/10/does-corporate-culture-drive-financial-performance, accessed August 2023; see also: JP Kotter and JL Heskett, *Corporate Culture and Performance* (Free Press, 2011)

35 For the scientists among you, forgive me for keeping things simple. Oxygen plays the role of an oxidiser in the combustion reaction, but any chemical species that can

replicate that role is a possible substitute for oxygen. R
Lunawat, 'Can fire burn when there's no oxygen?', *Science
ABC* (17 January 2022), www.scienceabc.com/nature/
can-fire-occur-non-oxygenated-reaction.html, accessed
August 2023

36   LE McLeod, 'Why Monster.com is failing and others will
follow', *Forbes* (5 November 2014), www.forbes.com/sites/
lisaearlemcleod/2014/11/05/why-monster-is-failing-and-
others-will-follow/?sh=fb5229047dbd, accessed July 2023

37   'What are the Santa Ana or Santana Winds?', *Los Angeles
Almanac* (no date), www.laalmanac.com/weather/we23.
php, accessed August 2023

38   M Gladwell, *Outliers* (Penguin, 2009)

39   R Aydin, 'How 3 guys turned renting air mattresses in their
apartment into a \$31 billion company, Airbnb', *Business
Insider* (20 September 2019), www.businessinsider.com/
how-airbnb-was-founded-a-visual-history-2016-2, accessed
August 2023

40   K Lyons, 'Airbnb lost millions in revenue due to the
coronavirus, IPO filing reveals', The Verge (16 November
2020), www.theverge.com/2020/11/16/21570416/airbnb-
coronavirus-pandemic-travel-hospitality, accessed July 2023

41   'Anglo American', Responsible Mining Index 2022,
https://2022.responsibleminingindex.org/en/
companies/151, accessed August 2023

42   M Hall, 'Facebook: Social network', *Britannica* (updated
25 August 2023), www.britannica.com/topic/Facebook,
accessed August 2023

43   This does not apply to industries where precision is
required (such as pharma, nuclear, etc). Yet the general
point remains. Don't try and build everything before you
understand what your customer wants. The ideal is to
build with and alongside your target market.

44   'Profile: Richard Branson', *Forbes* (no date – real-time data
correct as of 29 August 2023), www.forbes.com/profile/
richard-branson, accessed August 2023

45   J Polish, 'Genius network interview: Richard Branson'
(no date), http://joepolish.com/richardbranson/Genius-
Network-Richard-Branson-Interviewed-By-Joe-Polish.pdf,
accessed July 2023

46   C Argyris and D Schon, *Theory in practice: Increasing
professional effectiveness* (Jossey Bass, 1974)

47 CA O'Reilly and ML Tushman, *Lead and Disrupt: How to solve the innovator's dilemma* (Stanford Business Books, 2021)

48 D Rooke and WR Torbert, 'Seven transformations of leadership', *Harvard Business Review* (April 2015), https://hbr.org/2005/04/seven-transformations-of-leadership, accessed July 2023

49 'GDPR penalties and fines: What's the maximum fine in 2023?', IT Governance (no date), www.itgovernance.co.uk/dpa-and-gdpr-penalties, accessed August 2023

50 'Number of JD Wetherspoon pubs in the United Kingdom (UK) and Ireland from 2007 to 2022', Statista (2023), www.statista.com/statistics/641629/number-of-wetherspoon-pubs-united-kingdom-ireland, accessed August 2023

51 D Rooke and WR Torbert, 'Seven transformations of leadership', *Harvard Business Review* (April 2015), https://hbr.org/2005/04/seven-transformations-of-leadership, accessed July 2023

52 'Astro Teller: Captain of Moonshots', X (no date), https://x.company/team/astroteller, accessed August 2023

53 C Clifford, 'Bill Gates took solo "think weeks" in a cabin in the woods – why it's a great strategy', *CNBC Make It* (28 July 2019), www.cnbc.com/2019/07/26/bill-gates-took-solo-think-weeks-in-a-cabin-in-the-woods.html, accessed August 2023

54 D Rooke and WR Torbert, 'Seven transformations of leadership', *Harvard Business Review* (April 2015), https://hbr.org/2005/04/seven-transformations-of-leadership, accessed July 2023

55 'Exclusive: Julian Dunkerton and Jade Holland Cooper open up about Superdry', *Tatler* (20 April 2019), www.tatler.com/article/julian-dunkerton-superdry-interview, accessed July 2023

56 T Harford, 'A powerful way to unleash your creativity', TEDTalks (2019), https://timharford.com/2019/01/my-ted-talk-on-the-power-of-slow-motion-multitasking, accessed July 2023

57 Z Mejia, 'Billionaire Richard Branson shares 4 tips to turn your dreams into success', CNBC (29 August 2017), www.cnbc.com/2017/08/29/richard-branson-shares-4-tips-to-turn-your-dreams-into-success.html, accessed July 2023

58 A Boult, 'Could you follow Richard Branson's daily routine? 5am starts and 20 cups of tea a day', *The Telegraph*

(7 April 2017), www.telegraph.co.uk/men/the-filter/could-follow-richard-bransons-daily-routine-5am-starts-20-cups, accessed August 2023

59 WeQual Global was set up to help WeQual achieve its objective of achieving 50/50 gender equality at the top of the world's largest companies. The Executive level membership is for women at board, C-suite and VP levels. The Rising Leaders level supports mid-level managers. At the time of printing, over 300 globally listed organisations are represented, with members coming from every corner of the world. Regular think tanks (open to all leaders) seek to share global best practice on a range of business issues, including equality. For more information see wequal.com.

60 W Isaacson, *Steve Jobs: The Exclusive Biography* (Little Brown, 2011)

61 For those from a Christian background, meditation is akin to the Bible verse, 'Be still and know that I am God' (Psalm 46:10). See also Psalm 48:9: 'Within your temple, O God, we meditate on your unfailing love.'

62 S Suzuki, *Beginner's Mind: Informal talks on Zen meditation and practice* (Waterhill Inc, 1973)

63 Just Eat, *Just Eat plc Annual Report and Accounts 2018* (Just Eat plc, 2018), www.annualreports.co.uk/HostedData/AnnualReports/PDF/LSE_JE_2018.pdf, accessed August 2023; 'Equities: Just Eat Takeaway.com NV', *Financial Times* (no date – real-time data correct as of 29 August 2023), https://markets.ft.com/data/equities/tearsheet/profile?s=TKWY:AEX, accessed August 2023

64 E Berne, *Games People Play: The psychology of human relationships* (Penguin, 2010)

65 The dynamic between leaders and their followers is significantly impacted by the culture within which they interact. Some cultures are significantly more autocratic, requiring followers to simply follow instructions, whereas in others challenging instructions is celebrated. This book is written within the context of leaders within global organisations, and those who seek to disrupt the status quo regardless of culture. Beyond the scope of this book, a good starting place from which to understand cultural differences is Hofstede's Country Comparison Tool: www.hofstede-insights.com/country-comparison-tool.

66 R Hastings and E Meyer, *No Rules: Netflix and the culture of revolution* (Virgin Books, 2020)

67   Winnie exists, and is amazing – I've just changed her name.
68   C Post, B Lokshin and C Boone, 'Research: Adding women
     to the C-suite changes how companies think', *Harvard
     Business Review* (6 April 2021), https://hbr.org/2021/04/
     research-adding-women-to-the-c-suite-changes-how-
     companies-think, accessed August 2023
69   S Dixon-Fyle, K Dolan, V Hunt and S Prince, *Diversity Wins:
     How inclusion matters* (McKinsey, 2020), www.mckinsey.
     com/featured-insights/diversity-and-inclusion/diversity-
     wins-how-inclusion-matters, accessed August 2023
70   R Lorenzo, N Voigt, K Schetelig, A Zawadzki, I Welpe and P
     Brosi, 'The mix that matters: Innovation through diversity',
     BCG (26 April 2017), www.bcg.com/publications/2017/
     people-organization-leadership-talent-innovation-through-
     diversity-mix-that-matters, accessed August 2023
71   K Elsesser, 'Women aren't risk-averse, they just face
     consequences when they take risks', *Forbes* (29 April 2022),
     www.forbes.com/sites/kimelsesser/2022/04/29/women-
     arent-risk-averse-they-just-face-consequences-when-they-
     take-risks, accessed August 2023
72   C Post, B Lokshin and C Boone, 'Research: Adding women
     to the C-suite changes how companies think', *Harvard
     Business Review* (6 April 2021), https://hbr.org/2021/04/
     research-adding-women-to-the-c-suite-changes-how-
     companies-think, accessed August 2023
73   T Aabo and IC Giorici, 'Do female CEOs matter
     for ESG scores?', *Global Finance Journal*, 56 (2023),
     www.sciencedirect.com/science/article/pii/
     S1044028322000242#bb0255, accessed August 2023; AH
     Fischer, ME Kret and J Broekens, 'Gender differences
     in emotion perception and self-reported emotional
     intelligence: A test of the emotion sensitivity hypothesis',
     PLoS One, 13/1 (2018), e0190712, www.ncbi.nlm.nih.gov/
     pmc/articles/PMC5784910, accessed August 2023
74   L Christov-Moore, EA Simpson, G Coudé, K Grigaityte, M
     Iacoboni and PF Ferrari, 'Empathy: Gender effects in brain
     and behavior', *Neuroscience and Biobehavioral Reviews*, 46/4
     (2014), 604–627, www.sciencedirect.com/science/article/
     abs/pii/S0149763414002164, accessed August 2023
75   X Meng and P Zhu, 'Females' Social Responsibility: The impact
     of female executives on ESG performance' (February 2023),

www.researchgate.net/publication/368672949_Females'_
social_responsibility_the_impact_of_female_executives_
on_ESG_performance, accessed September 2023

76 'Only nine FTSE 100 companies headed by women, study
finds', Robert Half (21 March 2022), www.roberthalf.co.uk/
only-nine-ftse-100-companies-headed-women-study-finds,
accessed July 2023

77 T Phillips, 'Green Park Business Leaders Index 2021 | FTSE
100', Green Park (no date), www.green-park.co.uk/insight-
reports/green-park-business-leaders-index-2021-ftse-100/
accessed July 2023

78 P Sweet, 'FTSE 100 has "zero" black senior board
executives', Accountancy Daily (5 February 2021), www.
accountancydaily.co/ftse-100-has-zero-black-senior-board-
executives, accessed September 2023

79 E Hinchliffe, 'The number of women running global 500
businesses soars to an all-time high', *Fortune* (2 August
2021), https://fortune.com/2021/08/02/female-ceos-
global-500-fortune-500-cvs-karen-lynch-ping-an-jessica-tan,
accessed September 2023

80 'Women in Management (Quick Take)', Catalyst (1 March
2022), www.catalyst.org/research/women-in-management,
accessed July 2023

81 'Women in the Workplace, 2021', McKinsey & Company
and Lean In (2021), https://womenintheworkplace.com,
accessed July 2023

82 K Abouzahr, M Krentz, J Harthorne and F Brooks, 'Why
women-owned start-ups are a better bet', BCG (6 June
2016), www.bcg.com/publications/2018/why-women-
owned-startups-are-better-bet.aspx, accessed July 2023

83 K Scannell and A Morrow, 'Judge says Bankman-Fried
could "conceivably" have bail revoked', CNN (16 February
2023), https://edition.cnn.com/2023/02/16/business/ftx-
bankman-fried-bail-hearing/index.html, accessed July 2023

84 L He, 'Google's Secrets Of Innovation: Empowering Its
Employees', *Forbes* (29 March 2013), https://community.
mis.temple.edu/ruimis/files/2013/06/Googles-Secrets-
Of-Innovation-Empowering-Its-Employees.pdf, accessed
July 2023

85 V Lipman, 'The best sentence I ever read about managing
talent', *Forbes* (25 September 2018), www.forbes.com/sites/
victorlipman/2018/09/25/the-best-sentence-i-ever-read-
about-managing-talent/?sh=7e5f1f97cdfb, accessed July 2023

86 RE Johnson, M Venus, K Lanaj, C Mao and C Chang,
    'Leader identity as an antecedent of the frequency and
    consistency of transformational, consideration, and abusive
    leadership behaviours', *Journal of Applied Psychology*, 97/6
    (2012), 1262–1272, http://doi.org/10.1037/a0029043
87 I Fraser, *Shredded: Inside RBS, the bank that broke Britain*
    (Birlinn, 2014)
88 E Askeland and K Dorsey, 'Where are they now: What
    became of the 18 Royal Bank of Scotland directors who
    oversaw its demise?', *The Scotsman* (11 December 2011),
    www.scotsman.com/business/where-are-they-now-what-
    became-18-royal-bank-scotland-directors-who-oversaw-its-
    demise-2004424, accessed July 2023
89 A room at Anfield, home of Liverpool FC, which was a
    meeting place for coaching staff from the 1960s to the early
    '90s, where they regularly discussed the team and tactics.
90 'Nokia becomes Europe's biggest publicly listed company',
    Market Watch (7 December 1999), www.marketwatch.com/
    story/nokia-becomes-europes-biggest-publicly-listed-
    company, accessed September 2023
91 D Lee, 'Nokia: The rise and fall of a mobile giant',
    BBC News (3 September 2013), www.bbc.com/news/
    technology-23947212, accessed September 2023
92 E Lane, 'Nokia: Life after the fall of a mobile phone
    giant', BBC News (18 March 2016), www.bbc.com/news/
    business-35807556, accessed September 2023
93 A Hartung, 'A $7.6B Write-Off Is Never A Good Sign,
    Microsoft', *Forbes* (8 July 2015), www.forbes.com/sites/
    adamhartung/2015/07/08/a-7-6b-write-off-is-never-a-
    good-sign-microsoft, accessed September 2023
94 A Webb, 'The 11 sources of disruption every company
    must monitor', *MIT Sloan Management Review* (10 March
    2020), https://sloanreview.mit.edu/article/the-11-sources-
    of-disruption-every-company-must-monitor, accessed
    July 2023
95 B Perrigo, 'Elon Musk signs open letter urging AI labs to
    pump the brakes', *Time* (29 March 2023), https://time.
    com/6266679/musk-ai-open-letter, accessed July 2023
96 ME Porter, 'How competitive forces shape strategy',
    Harvard Business Review, 57/2 (1979), 137–145, https://
    hbr.org/1979/03/how-competitive-forces-shape-strategy,
    accessed July 2023

97 J Saba, 'Review: Blockbuster's demise had many culprits', Reuters (16 April 2021), www.reuters.com/breakingviews/ review-blockbusters-demise-had-many-culprits-2021-04-16, accessed September 2023

98 The British branch of the F W Woolworth Company (which had been founded in Pennsylvania), F W Woolworth & Co Ltd, was founded by Frank Woolworth in Liverpool, England on 5 November 1909. It went on to become the Woolworths Group.

99 'What has happened to Woolworths' stores 10 years after closure?', BBC News (19 November 2018), www.bbc.com/ news/business-46259048, accessed September 2023

100 C de Looper, 'One man's shiny new Samsung Galaxy Note 7 exploded while charging', Digital Trends (24 August 2016), www.digitaltrends.com/mobile/samsung-galaxy-note-7-exploded, accessed September 2023

101 SA O'Brien, 'Samsung: Don't freak out about exploding Galaxy S7s', CNN Business (21 November 2016), https:// money.cnn.com/2016/11/21/technology/samsung-galaxy-s7/index.html, accessed September 2023

102 'Samsung Operating Profit Plunges 30% In Wake Of Note 7 Fiasco', BBC News (27 October 2016), www.bbc.co.uk/ news/business-37784079, accessed September 2023

103 R McAllister, 'Crisis Recover Case Study: Samsung 18 months on from the explosive S7 Note', Continuity Central (16 February 2018), https://continuitycentral.com/index. php/news/business-continuity-news/2684-crisis-recovery-case-study-samsung-18-months-on-from-the-explosive-s7-note, accessed September 2023

104 D McRaney, 'Survivorship bias', You Are Not So Smart (23 May 2013), https://youarenotsosmart. com/2013/05/23/survivorship-bias, accessed July 2023

105 Abraham Wald was born in Hungary in 1902, the son of a Jewish baker. He spent his childhood studying equations, eventually working his way up through academia. He escaped the Nazis by fleeing to the US from Hungary in 1938 (and lost all his family at Auschwitz bar one brother). Soon after Wald arrived in the United States, he joined the Applied Mathematics Panel, whose role was to support the war effort using maths.

106 N Lomas, 'UK report spotlights the huge investment gap facing diverse founders', Tech Crunch (2 November 2020),

https://techcrunch.com/2020/11/02/uk-report-spotlights-the-huge-investment-gap-facing-diverse-founders, accessed July 2023

107 MC White, 'Detailed Biographies of Apollo I Crew – Gus Grissom', NASA (updated August 4 2006), https://history.nasa.gov/Apollo204/zorn/grissom.htm, accessed July 2023; DK Slayton and M Cassutt, *Deke! US Manned Space: from Mercury to the Shuttle* (St Martin's Press, 1994)

108 E Langer, 'Richard Gordon, astronaut of Gemini and Apollo missions, dies at 88', *The Washington Post* (8 November 2017), www.washingtonpost.com/local/obituaries/richard-gordon-astronaut-of-gemini-and-apollo-missions-dies-at-88/2017/11/08/a38d8d04-c3fe-11e7-aae0-cb18a8c29c65_story.html, accessed July 2023

109 Gordon set an altitude record of 1,369 kilometres (851 mi), which still stands as the highest-apogee Earth orbit ever. He also logged a total of 315 hours and 53 minutes in space, of which 2 hours and 41 minutes were spent outside the aircraft.

110 'International Classification of Diseases 10th Revision', World Health Organization (no date), https://icd.who.int/browse10/2019/en#/Z73.0, accessed September 2023

111 L Kwoh, 'When the CEO burns out', Harvard Medical School (7 May 2013), https://hms.harvard.edu/news/when-ceo-burns-out, accessed July 2023

112 K Makortoff, '"I suffered anxiety": Monzo founder on the pressures of running a digital bank', *The Guardian* (30 January 2021), www.theguardian.com/money/2021/jan/30/monzo-founder-digital-bank-tom-blomfield-covid-19, accessed July 2023

113 JO Prochaska and CC DiClemente, 'The transtheoretical approach', in JC Norcross and MR Goldfried, *Handbook of Psychotherapy Integration*, 2nd edition (Oxford University Press, 2005), 147–171

114 T Gale, 'Why Don't CEOs Want Executive Coaching?', Transform (11 April 2016), https://transforminc.com/2016/04/why-dont-ceos-want-executive-coaching, accessed September 2023

115 JB Stewart, 'A CEO's support system, aka husband', *The New York Times* (4 November 2011), www.nytimes.com/2011/11/05/business/a-ceos-support-system-a-k-a-husband.html, accessed July 2023

116 For further reading on how large organisations can continue to innovate, read *The Innovator's Dilemma* by Clayton Christensen and *Lead and Disrupt: How to solve the innovator's dilemma*, 2nd edition by Charles O'Reilly and Michael Tushman.

117 G Chen, 'Top 5 tips for Chinese entrepreneurs from Lenovo's Liu Chuanzhi', *South China Morning Post* (29 June 2015), www.scmp.com/lists/article/1829082/top-5-tips-chinese-entrepreneurs-lenovos-liu-chuanzhi, accessed July 2023

118 M Durot, 'Warren Buffet has now given record $48 billion to charity', *Forbes* (14 June 2022), www.forbes.com/sites/mattdurot/2022/06/14/warren-buffett-just-gave-another-4-billion-to-charity, accessed July 2023

Further Reading

Berne, E, *Games People Play: The psychology of human relationships* (Penguin, 2010).
Introduces transactional analysis to explain how human relationships develop and deteriorate.

Brown, B, *Dare to Lead* (Random House, 2018).
Offers research-driven insights into developing courage-based leadership, exploring the ability to step up, put yourself out there and lean into courage.

Cain, S, *Quiet: The power of introverts in a world that can't stop talking* (Penguin, 2012).
A compelling journey through the science and history of introversion, offering invaluable insights on the power and potential of quiet individuals.

Christensen, CM, *The Innovator's Dilemma* (Harvard
Business Review Press, 2016).
Delves into how successful, outstanding companies
can do everything 'right' and yet still lose market
dominance, introducing the idea of disruptive
innovation. A great read on those companies that
are able to innovate from within.

Collins, J, *Good to Great: Why some companies
make the leap and others don't* (Random House
Business, 2001).
Based on a five-year research project, Collins
delves into what it takes for companies to go
from good to great, providing practical advice for
leadership.

Dweck, CS, *Mindset: The new psychology of success*
(Ballantine Books, 2013).
Examines the concept of 'mindset' and how our
beliefs about our abilities can impact our success.

Gladwell, M, *Outliers: The story of success*
(Penguin, 2008).
Explores the factors that decide the difference
between successful and unsuccessful people,
arguing that individual merit is less important
than our surroundings.

Goleman, D, *Working With Emotional Intelligence*
(Bloomsbury, 2009).

Explains why emotional intelligence can be more important than IQ and how you can use your emotions to your advantage.

Grant, A, *Think Again: The power of knowing what you don't know* (Virgin Digital, 2021).
Encourages readers to question their own convictions and adapt their beliefs upon learning new information, fostering an innovative and open mindset.

Hastings, R and Meyer, E, *No Rules: Netflix and the culture of reinvention* (Virgin Digital, 2020).
Provides a behind-the-scenes look at the culture of one of the most successful tech companies, offering insights into leadership, creativity and innovation.

Lencioni, P, *The Five Dysfunctions of a Team* (Jossey-Bass, 2007).
Outlines the root causes of politics and dysfunction on the teams where you work, and the keys to overcoming them.

Moore, GA, *Crossing the Chasm: Marketing and selling high-tech products to mainstream customers,* 3rd edition (Collins Business Essentials, 2013).
A key resource for understanding the specifics of tech product marketing and how to effectively reach more customers.

O'Reilly, CA and Tushman, ML, *Lead and Disrupt: How to solve the innovator's dilemma*, 2nd edition (Stanford Business Books, 2021).

A guide to strategic leadership for those in charge of large, complex organisations who aim to maintain innovation in the face of disruptive forces.

Sandberg, S, *Lean In: Women, work, and the will to lead* (Virgin Digital, 2013).

A must-read for anyone interested in gender equality, this book addresses key issues and offers practical advice for women aiming for leadership roles.

Sinek, S, *Start With Why* (Penguin, 2011).

Offers valuable insight into the power of inspiration and motivation, suggesting that effective leaders can inspire cooperation, trust and change if they start by asking 'why'.

Syed, M, *Rebel Ideas: The power of diverse thinking* (John Murray, 2019).

Reveals how diversity of thought can stimulate innovation and solve some of the world's most intractable problems.

Tzu, S, *The Art of War* (Capstone, 2010).

While ancient, its strategies about leadership, decision-making and dealing with competition remain highly relevant for business leaders.

Acknowledgements

My wonderful parents, I honour and love you both.

Dad, in a strange way, I wrote this book for you. I have always watched, learned from and yearned for your success as you pursued the difference you wanted to make. I had the benefit of experiencing the highs and lows afforded by the opportunities to lead under you, and I gained rich insights from the diverse leaders you and Mum invited into our family home and from those we visited.

Mum, being the recipient of your unwavering love and support is the greatest honour. I can't tell you how proud I am of the day you simply listened to me when I needed you to, and of how you didn't leave your career simply because you reached retirement age. You are an inspiration to all women everywhere.

To my daughters, who taught me what it is to be a dad. You have both enriched my life in countless ways and made it more meaningful. You fill me with immeasurable pride, regardless of what you do or don't do. I love you both. My sincerest wish for you is a long, purposeful and fulfilled life.

To my business partner, Katie Litchfield, who deserves immense recognition. It is an absolute joy to work alongside you as we strive to find global solutions to global problems. Despite the challenges we've faced, our shared journey has been nothing short of inspirational. I can't wait for the next chapter (and for your book!).

To the growing team at WeQual, my heartfelt thanks go out to you. Similarly, to the leaders of both fledgling and established companies who have chosen to work with me over the years, both before and now at WeQual, I am continuously humbled and energised by your passion, purpose and remarkable ability to effect change.

Alison Northcott deserves a special mention for her invaluable help in researching the backstories for all of the contributors in this book.

I would also like to extend my sincere thanks to my ghostwriter, who masterfully wove my interviews into a manuscript that had languished on a digital shelf for four years.

To the rest of my family, and every individual who has been a part of my journey, I only stand where I do today thanks to you.

Last but not least, I would like to acknowledge the leaders I interviewed for this book. Your drive, your tenacity and your humanity have had an indelible impact on me. I hope that I have successfully encapsulated and conveyed some of your remarkable essence, which serves as a shining example for us all to follow. Thank you.

The Author

 Mark Bateman is a visionary disruptor, corporate adviser and executive coach with a keen focus on leadership development. With decades of experience in business, he has navigated the peaks and troughs of industry, making his mark as a successful entrepreneur and then selling his own tech consulting firm. Since then, Mark has dedicated himself to the development of leaders worldwide, amassing over 3,000 hours of executive coaching, and making impactful contributions to some of the world's top global companies.

As the CEO of WeQual, Mark is leading a movement that champions gender equality in corporate leadership roles, demonstrating the compelling case that balanced leadership teams drive better business results across every metric. Through the WeQual Awards and Global Membership initiatives, Mark continues to identify and support outstanding women leaders on their journey to the top.

His commitment to fostering leadership isn't limited to the boardroom. Mark's academic achievements, including a master's in leadership coaching and mentoring, underscore his comprehensive understanding of human psychology and the transformative power of leadership.

Beyond his professional endeavours, Mark is a proud father of two grown-up daughters, an avid traveller and a fitness enthusiast. Based in Malta, he frequently travels to London and other nations, reflected in his global perspective on leadership.

His latest endeavour, *Disruptive Leadership: Using Fire to Drive Purposeful Change*, is a result of four years of intensive research, interviews with global CEOs and senior leaders and a lifetime of experience. This book captures the essence of Mark's unique approach to leadership – fanning the flames of disruption to incite significant, beneficial change. His passion for unleashing the potential of leaders is captured on every page, making it an essential read for those ready to disrupt, transform and lead in the twenty-first century.

in linkedin.com/in/batemanmark

⊕ www.mark-bateman.com

⊕ www.wequal.com

Made in United States
North Haven, CT
25 January 2024